Lucy Cavendish

Artwork by Selina Fenech

Wild Wisdom of the Faery Oracle

BLUE ANGEL
PUBLISHING

Wild Wisdom of the Faery Oracle

Published by Blue Angel Publishing
80 Glen Tower Drive, Glen Waverley,
Victoria, Australia 3150
Phone: +61 3 9574 7776
Fax: +61 3 9574 7772
E-mail: tonicarmine@optusnet.com.au
Website: www.blueangelonline.com

Card messages written by Lucy Cavendish
Artwork Copyright © Selina Fenech
Design © 2009 Blue Angel Gallery
Edited by Tanya Graham

ISBN: 978-0-98055504-2

Faeries, come take me out of this dull world,
For I would ride with you upon the wind,
Run on the top of the disheveled tide,
And dance upon the mountains like a flame.

~William Butler Yeats, *The Land of Heart's Desire*

Contents

Once upon a time, they say... *As if there was only that one time, as if it has long passed into the fields of long-ago. But what if that Once Upon A Time is now, eternal, and what if your time to be in that faerytale place has returned . . . because in that once upon a time world, that place of enchantment, you and I could move between the worlds with ease and trust. And when we grew tired and older, and were heavy of heart, we would take ourselves to a tree and lie down upon our mother, the earth. All trees are sacred, but this one was older and wiser than even the oaks. A sacred thorn tree, under whose branches we would go to sleep, and dream of bright realms. A place where faeries dwelled, and healed and charmed us back to health and wholeness, where the heavy weights that were bound about our heart were unlocked, one by one, with faery keys. And how we laughed, and feasted, and loved while in this realm. And when we were whole, and wild, and healed again, we awoke under that same tree, and knew that we were returned from a realm where time has a different meaning. Where life has enchantment. Where flowers speak and animals teach, and where our faery kin had rewoven the energies of the world into shining, beautiful shapes.*

For the truth is that our faery kin have for aeons cleansed and brightened the skies, have whispered 'grow' to the crops that fed us, and shielded the old forests from the gaze of those who would hunt them for their wood. And when we had been given the key to the faery realm, we too were strong in body, mind and soul, and we danced under the moonlight and were bathed in the bliss of life. We weaved the energy between the stones, we knew how to shape time and we allowed ourselves to go into the faery realms to be restored, made whole and clean again. For there we can rest, and be revived again to our whole self. And when we were strong in our relationship with our faery-kin, oh how we shone! For we were bright, and we glowed with our connection to the source.

And then . . . well, and then.

It is time. It is that Once Upon a Time again. Time to return to our relationship with the wild places, the wild ones, the faeries, and our wildish selves. For as we do, miracles of healing will occur. Just as faeries cleanse and purify the water, the air, the earth, the fire and the spirit, when we reweave our sacred alliance with the faery realms, we too begin to heal. From our sadness. Our loneliness. From our souls that cry out for the poetry that is the soul of the world.

If you yearn to shine once again, if you wish to reclaim the wildish self who lives at the heart of you, who knows how to be well, to be happy, to be whole. . . if you wish to clear illness, guilt, and untruths from your life and truly, deeply heal and transform, then this deck is your set of keys to the faery realm, and there you will be reborn.

This oracle deck is your key to those wildish places where not only can you be restored, but you will find sacred union, connection, true health and wholeness. Be blessed, enter this enchanted place and be prepared for your heart to fill, your soul to sing and your body to fill with the energy of the wild green world. Take the key. And keep it safe. And know you are welcome to return to these realms, and come home to us again, beloved.

Welcome to the magick of the faery realm: a place of healing, laughter, physical rebirth and restored belief. When you enter this realm, be prepared for change to come, time to be reshaped, events to take on different destinies and the ecstasy of being alive to flow through your veins. You may dance under the stars and call out to the moon – anything is possible, and desirable, when you have been touched by the faeries, and restored to your true, wildish self!

Who are the Faeries?

Faeries are the intoxicating, beautiful, wild and playful feminine shapeshifters. They are the protectors of Mother Gaia's sacred wild places – from valleys to rivers, to mountaintops and seabeds, to beyond her atmosphere and into the starry skies above. Faeries are etheric starfire and earthly greenings, and they protect and heal all that is in physical form.

Faeries are many-named, but the not-so magical word 'fairy' has its root in the Latin *fatum*, which means destiny, with the added shade of an enchanted fate. An early version of their name was spelt 'fayerie', which refers to being under the spell of a faery! From that word sprung forth names like fairy, fair folk, pherie, fees, fey, the fae and the fions. Their various forms are called knockers, boggarts, pookas, sidhe (pronounced shee) the Tuatha de Danaan, the Tylweth Teg, gnomes, elves, pixies, brownies, stray-sods and of course, the good folk.

Though they are indeed good folk, extensive, fear-based and threatening propaganda by the Church conspired to give faeries a very bad name. When they were not being trivialised, they were feared! And yet the truth of the faeries is that they are strong and powerful beings of form and light. They bridge the celestial and the terrestrial, embodying and enspiriting completely the dictum 'as above so below'. They create from within – 'as within so without'. They teach us shapeshifting, weather changing, keening our sense so they can work and communicate over time and space. They use the healing arts of herb and touch, divination, manifestation, creativity, music, art, writing and sensual, ecstatic rites. Their powerful sexuality is one of the reasons that the Churchists of many religions forbid interaction with the faeries.

Those who danced with them under the moonlight were called witches, a word which simply means to bend and change, and has an additional meaning of wise. Thus witches change things according to their wisdom, manifesting for the earth's highest good! Faeries and witches alike were accused of terrible activities, and these rumours were spread to create fear in the hearts of those who were closest to the faery. The pagans, or people who lived in the countryside, and the heathens, those who lived on the heath, believed in faeries long after most of us were told they existed only between the ears and on the pages of slightly silly stories. But many people mistrusted the faeries. Changeling children were said to be nested, cuckoo-like, within human families, and human children were said to be stolen.

There has long been exchange and communication 'tween the worlds of human and faery, where once the veils were softer and sheerer than they presently are. We have loved each other long, and feared each other for such a short time. If we can love each other again, what bliss there shall be, what freedom, what creativity and joy! What health and strength and spirit of place shall return, and how happy and well we shall all be.

But we have much work to do. For they in truth have far more to fear from us, than we from them.

You see, faeries are co-dependent on the health of their natural environment. Sluggish rivers choking with blue-green algae and overwhelmed with pesticides and fertilizer runoff are protected by faeries whose health is in turn compromised by mankind's tragic historical interferences with the natural world. As the faery's divine purpose is to protect her chosen element or animal, her health is essential to her being able to fulfill her divine mission. So we goddesses and elementals in human form have a twofold reason to help heal our beautiful green and blue planet. We can do this by being gentle, strong warriors, speaking our truth about the sanctity of the mother's wild places, her forests, oceans, deserts and mountaintops. All of her is sacred, and all of her needs our protection, more now than ever before.

Being elemental, meaning they exist between the worlds, the way in which the divine faeries communicate with we humans can take many forms, some of which may seem unusual to those of us beginning to explore interacting with those who are other than human. Their messages are whispered on the wind, transmitted through intuitive feelings and hunches and seen in visions. When all else fails, the faeries reach out to us by calling us to a place, then speaking to us with images and fables through our dreams. They are creative, and work closely with artists and people who use the right side of their brain. Sometimes, for humans who have worked with them, or from whom they have a request to make, they will become manifest before them – utterly real, and utterly physical. We can then speak with them clearly, and wonder at our ability to be a part of this so often hidden world. Faeries also communicate with us through the sensual arts: they love to hug and to embrace us, to stroke our hair, and to help us shed tears that have been dammed up inside us. Sometimes they fall in love with humans – and oh so often, humans have fallen in love with them!

So, we have the beautiful mystery of the faeries shapeshifting ability being so strong that they can appear to become as we are – flesh. A distinctive characteristic of the faeries is this ease with which they can move between their human-like self, and their elemental physical vessel. This allows them intense and physical relationships with the Gods, humans and other elementals. In fact, many humans have this magick in their own bloodlines as a result of an ancient – or perhaps more recent – encounter with an elemental.

So, the faery can become as one with the tree she has been made the protectress of. If that tree is harmed or suffers, so does the faery who protects it. If faeries wish to make contact with a human, they will do so – more often subtly than through outright transformation and clear interaction. They are very shy, wild creatures. If they need to hide from us, they can easily do this by combining their physical matter with that of the tree, the flower, the bird on the wing…

All faeries tend to be "classed" by us, for clear understanding, by their chosen environment which they protect and interact with. There are various

11

types of water faeries, just as there are various bodies of water. Varying faeries care for the trees. Others, tall and "angelic" in form, care for the mountains. Others watch over the meadows. Wherever nature breathes out her rapture, there are faeries caring for every living creature.

Though they are ancient and long-lived indeed, faeries are not immortal. They are absolutely divine, but the length of their sometimes very ancient lives depends on the health of the environment in which they dwell. Imagine the plight of the faeries as the forests are felled, or as a tanker spills its poison ooze into the ocean, or as toxins are dumped into a body of natural water.

> *Hand in hand, with faery grace,*
> *Will we sing, and bless this place.*
> William Shakespeare, *A Midsummer Night's Dream*

12

Blessed by the Faeries:

How to Communicate and Heal by Working with the Faery Realm

Faeries are wild healers of both the earth and celestial realms, beings who are less purely spirit than angels, who are less solid in form than humans. They are with you when you garden, smell a flower, feel a breeze, meditate in the outdoors first thing in the morning, bathe in the ocean, and step gently over a faery ring of mushrooms. When you gaze up at the stars, make a wish on a new moon, and walk towards the end of a rainbow. They come to you in your dreams, reach you via your emotions, and they encourage you to reconnect with the wild things. And when you reconnect with the wild, a part of you that has stayed silent too long finds its song, and begins to sing again.

Faeries are sometimes whimsically hard to trace. They would rather let you know of their presence with a gust of air, a faery breath whooshing on your cheek, or a bouncing leaf, vibrating up and down on a tree when there is no breath of wind about! They are predominantly invisible to many people's eyes, and yet they are present. As the world is wild at heart, so are they always with us. They will whisper to you of taking the day off work, running away and joining the circus, laughing during a serious speech and flicking rubber bands at bores!

But beneath their well-deserved reputation as mischief-making unpredictables, we often forget that at their wild heart is the nature and calling of the healer. They, after all, are the weavers of Source, which winds its way into every flower and tree and every sod of earth. Every root of tree has its gnome, its earth dweller nurturing all. The gnomes tend the underworld regions, and often come above to care for animals. They are in charge of transformation, the management of earth alchemy, as they oversee the business of breaking down and recreation.

The faeries of the herbs and flowers are skilled and insightful healers, who are the intuitive medical geniuses, knowing as they do a great deal about herbs, time, restoration and the power of nature. But more than that, because they are so in tune with their song, and can hear our unsung vibrations, they know what we need in order to be sung back to health.

They are musicians and artists, creating spun silver webs with dewdrops, wands with icicles, dancing intricate movements that are unplanned and never to be repeated. They create, and recreate again and again, and they follow no recipe, for they, remember, are wild at heart.

Who can Connect with Faeries?

We all can, as long as a trace of our own song, and our own wild hearts beat somewhere within. It is not silly, or childish to be a faery-believer. To say and do so means you open yourself up to the possibilities of magick and worlds beyond what can be seen and explained by what we call science. Yet, science and magick are so connected. The faeries taught the healers to use the bark of the willow to create aspirin; the faeries teach the herblore that is at the root of much of modern medicine. They whispered and worked with the great healer centaur, Chiron, who brought the healing arts to the planet from the realms above and below. And they dance between and within the planes. They are anarchic and wild, and seem dangerous to many who want their healing predictable, safe and orderly. But the faeries are not so. And nor, at your wild heart, are you.

I believe in everything until it's disproved. So I believe in faeries, the myths, dragons. It all exists, even if it's in your mind. Who's to say that dreams and nightmares aren't as real as the here and now?
John Lennon

Why Connect with Faeries?

To pass their lives on fountains and on flowers,
and never know the weight of human hours.
Lord Byron

We have been told many fearful stories about the faeries, but those of us with wild hearts have kept the lore alive. While it is not true that without our belief, they die (they cannot – as long as there are wild things, there will be faeries) but without belief, it is we who cannot see, and thus a little of us dies. And to halt the belief in faeries, who, after all, do not follow rigid rules, follow one after the other, nor do they stay silent when told, the people of the churches told stories of baby-stealing, of faery-bolts that would afflict suffers. If you were to go to faeryland, you were warned to never partake of their food or drink, lest you remain there forever. The abduction stories certainly did their work, but the belief did not die.

Faery Energy

The faeries teach us that we can be restored and revived. That we can feel and grow actually younger, healthier, stronger, happier again, if we give ourselves over to faery-reality and know that the unseen is nevertheless there and has great power. When we work with faeries, we work with an energy that is a kind of mystic ecology. We no longer waste our personal sovereignity or power, and we learn how to transmute what feels and seems negative, both within and without, into something useful and of service. In this way we stay well, young, and healthy.

This is not to say we wish to "look young" and deny the crone within, nor that stage of our lives. But we wish to embrace this stage with vitality and richness – that is the power of faery.

Faery Beliefs

While so many seem to feel that faeries are once-upon-a-time-beings, faery beliefs are no ancient thing. In 2000 in County Clare in Ireland, the birthplace of some of my matriarchal ancestors, construction of a motorway was halted thanks to the protest of a seanachai, or storyteller. He pointed out that one of the "obstacles" due to be cleared to make way for the serpent of cement was a white thorn bush – a faery tree. Eddie Linehan explained that the white thorn tree was a resting place for many faeries traveling on the faery roads from Clare to Galway. Mr Linehan was not only concerned for the faery path and the sacred tree, but also for the oasis of calm that the tree was for the faeries on their walks cross country, singing the land back into health. It was also a portal for lonely and tired humans and he knew that if it came down, there would likely be an increase in accidents at the same spot on the road.

The bush was not only spared, it has become a sacred place, where visitors travel for miles and miles to leave a gift for the faeries.

Ireland's faeries are so very alive – even members of the royal family know their power. In the 1950s, Britain's Princess Margaret and Lord Snowdon were in Ireland, going west – the direction where faeries are so often to be found. They had been informed that it was considered impolite and disrespectful not to get out and chat to the faeries that lived underneath the bridge. So they did so, and then continued to travel westward, where they would have been blessed by so many faeries for their courtesy.

The iron tongue of midnight hath told twelve;
lovers to bed; 'tis almost faery time.
William Shakespeare

Faery places have special attributes. Time seems to slow, the air can lighten and become sweeter, more misty, and the entire atmosphere can alter to become a dreamscape. At Mahon Falls in Ireland, there is another faery tree. It stands on a hill. If you stop your car at the bottom of the hill, your car will continue to move – uphill – towards the tree. The same occurs within large stone circles, where the resonance is still slow and languid, where the heartbeat of the earth is still somewhere at 7 hertz, rather than the 11 it is at in cities and built-up areas, creating and accelerating our pace of life. In these faery stands of trees, where only one may remain, or stones, which may have been cracked and burnt over the years by fearful people wanting to mount a pre-emptive strike on nature's spirits, time paces herself differently. She is circular, rhythmic, dreamier, more imaginative, and creates wonderful opportunities for time travel and communing with nature's greatest healers.

Within faery rings (of trees, flowers, stones, mounds, natural creations of any kind) there may also be a different climate. Outside the ring it may rain; within, it may be sunshine and rainbows. The world within the ring is indeed a world within a world, a world of manifestation and magic, where things are indeed different, and we are enchanted.

Faeries are true healers. Faeries can alter the course of your physical healing swiftly, sweetly and powerfully. Do not underestimate them. They will not be felled by anyone declaring their disbelief, or by people taking away the wild places. They can only be felled by the disappearance of the wild self: within you, nature, animals and the elements. When we ask them for physical healing, they truly get to work.

Why is this, when they can be so capricious? Because most often, people facing illness or true hardship have reached a stage where they have honesty and their intent is true. They are often at a point where they are walkers between the worlds. They are filled with Source, and all the things that do not matter so much to the faeries probably matter less to you when something deep and strange happens to alter your physical world. People with illnesses are transformed by the experience. They gain deep wisdom, and know what is important. When we reach that place, whether through physical illness, an accident, cancer, depression or losing someone dear, the faeries know you have touched the very core of yourself, and you know what it is to be alive, and to face death.

So this is where they can enter. At the point where our mask drops away, and we realise that they are not fantasy, but reality – we can see them, and oh, how they can see into our heart of hearts.

Faeries teach us techniques that can transform what seems negative and harmful to our health into a more earthy and pure form that can heal. We can build up these stores of energy, and reclaim our innate ability to transform energy.

You do not need to be in crisis to reach them though. They will help with caring for the health, wellbeing and happiness of the animals you share your home with. They adore animals – the gnomes in particular nurse and heal all animal beings – including ourselves! Connecting with faeries is highly transformative; it is not childish or "silly", fluffy or vapid to see and hear them. Faery healing is powerful, and connected to our spirit, and is a wilder, more etheric form of shamanic lore. Faery healing is true earth and sky healing, it is deeply personal, immersing you in your own self and truths, and can transform physical aches, pains, even cancers and illnesses with its magickal healing powers.

How to Work with the Faeries

I think that people who can't believe in faeries aren't worth knowing.
Tori Amos

People who identify as fey, who know they have faery blood, or who connect strongly with the faery realms, often feel like outsiders: like orphans and wanderers, misfits and seekers. They believe that much of what others call reality is anything but, and they know that which is unseen by human eyes is often more real than that which we can oh-so-easily see, touch, taste, feel and hear. We resist boundaries and being defined and confined by others. People who connect with faery often change their lives many times within the one lifetime. They adore the poetic and romantic approach to life that sees its mystery being lived deeply. We are beings of faery energy.

Faeries work with people who are honest with themselves, and who are ready to be themselves. People who seem to have a natural affinity for working with faeries are often unconventional, artistic, love wildlife and the outdoors, lose track of time easily, daydream, are deeply affected by music, and have a wonderful sense of humour and delight. They can be moody and gloomy, too, at times, and are often more easily affected than others by addictive substances; including caffeine, chocolate and certain foods. Alcohol and drugs are certainly toxic for them. They fall in love deeply, and they do suffer heartbreak. They are also, interestingly, deep and passionate lovers, but they adore their freedom, so they are often conflicted about relationships. It can be hard to get them to "commit", though they are generally very loyal.

People who work with faeries often link very well to a group of faeries they may share blood with. Tall, slender and pale folk may have within them blood from the Tuatha. Those of us who have darker hair, and are earthier in form, are perhaps of the pixies. And those of us who can sing well – well, we have more than a touch of the Tylweth Teg!

When you have thought and felt that out, and if you feel you are willing to walk the wilder path, to be wholly yourself and to be less society's, faeries can begin to work with you, and create immense healing. They are not servants nor are they slaves; if you ask them to conduct trivial business for you, with no "heart" in it, and with no gratitude, they will not entrust their wild magicks to you.

That is not to say they will not assist with the small things. Being often small themselves, they know it is not the size of the quest that matters. But if a thing is done without clear and pure intent, if it is done out of selfish and lazy needs, and if it is not honestly done, the faeries will not intervene. For how would anything born of such intent assist you, truly?

Firstly, make an offering to the wild beings of faery. This will let them see you have integrity and are willing to take action.

You create your relationship because you are connected to the vital creative power of nature. They grant wishes: beauty, foresight, wisdom and healing. And they come to those who are in tune with nature and who care for her. So, to manifest working with the faeries, get in touch with your own natural surroundings.

*Have a clean up day. Pick up litter etc. Build this into your life so that you are naturally helping, rather than doing it one day, then feeling you have done enough. The faeries understand you cannot be at it at all times, but they also know that being faery cannot be segregated into a part of your life.

*Make a donation to a wildlife project, either of your time, some money, or your support.

*Join a revegetation project.

*Work with natural ways of cleaning your home and learn more about companion planting and permaculture.

*Care for your garden.

*Grow herbs, particularly the wild herb thyme.

*Hang bells or windchimes.

*Use candlelight rather than harsh overhead electric light.

*Create a faery door.

*Make a magical wand. Never pluck this from a living tree. Ask and the tree may give to you what you desire. Or, look for fallen wood gifted already to you from the trees!

*Let the faeries know what you are doing with the garden, the lawn, or trees. Have a chat with them and tell them when you would like to mow lawns…if you must mow them!

*If in faery realms, DO eat their food, and drink their wine. It is healing, and can amplify your own talents and skills. It is also very physically healing; others will marvel at your energy!

*If you take a faery lover, know that this relationship can be very enticing, and it is important to remain grounded physically in this world, too. It may not be forever, but it will be forever beautiful.

When to Work with the Faeries

Many faeries are far more likely to emerge from their secret hideaways and hidden places during the festivals of Beltane and Samhain, when the veil between the worlds is at its thinnest, as well as the other magical seasons of the earth and the sacred moon days. So if we observe and keep and honor these blessed festivals of the Goddess and her celestial and earthly events, we will open ourselves up to wonderful, magical encounters and interactions with the faeries.

New Moon (Wishes come true)

Full Moon (High tide of psychic power)

Outside, or within a dwelling with plants and natural forms.

Twilight (Reflection)

Dawn (Anticipation)

Sunrise (Joy)

Sunset (Gratitude)

These liminal times all help us be walkers between the worlds and the magick of faery is most tangible when the light is in-between. The festivals of the wheel of the year where faeries are most out and about are listed below. The doorways to the world of the fae swing wide open and welcome you in at these magickal times.

Litha: Summer solstice. Falls between December 20-23 (Southern hemisphere) / June 21-23 (Northern hemisphere). This is sometimes called the festival of the faeries! It brings slow warm and fun days, joy, laughter and reveling. (Galactic portal)

Lughnasad: February 1-2 (Southern hemisphere) / August 1-2 (Northern hemisphere). The first harvest. Watch for faeries bringing in grain and corn, and making faery breads and sharing them. Bring in your own harvest, and be grateful for all you have, for then the faeries will bring you even more blessings. (Gaia portal)

Mabon: Autumn Equinox. March 20-23 (Southern hemisphere) / September 20-23 (Northern hemisphere). Watch for the faeries bringing in their harvest, and make wishes for your abundance and your life force to hold during the winter's colder times. Watch for the faeries bringing frost, delicately weaving fractal geometry into endless patterns to remind us of the sacred cycle of time and life. (Galactic portal)

Samhain: April 30 - May 1 (Southern hemisphere) / October 31 - November 1 (Northern hemisphere). Your faery blood will sing at this time, and you will have great insights into your ancestry, even your own faery bloodline.(Gaia portal)

Yule: Winter solstice. June 20-23 (Southern hemisphere) / December 21-23 (Northern hemisphere). Significant for the Scandinavian faeries of Elfthame (elf-home), Yule is the celebration rebirth of the Sun God. Look for faeries welcoming in the Sun Goddess, Dragonfae being and their Queen, Grian, at this time. You may also see a great deal of golden energy out of the corner of your eye. These are fae spreading sunlight's power. (Galactic portal)

Imbolc: August 1-2 (Southern hemisphere) / February1-2 (Northern hemisphere). The celebration of spring and the maiden, and baby faeries are to be found everywhere. Leave them out some milk, so faery mothers have sustenance, and know you love them too. Welcome in Bride by lighting a candle and making a faery wish upon it. (Gaia portal)

Ostara: Spring Equinox. September 20-23 (Southern hemisphere) / March 20-23 (Northern hemisphere). This is the time to plant your seeds and ask the faery Prince for what you wish! Your dreams and wishes fall upon faery ears willing and ready to hear and help them come true. Help baby animals, and rid yourself of any toxins in your cleaning products or cosmetics you may still be using at this time. These show the faeries you are serious!

Beltane: October 31 - November 1 (Southern hemisphere) / April 30 - May 1 (Northern hemisphere). Watch for the faery Kings and Queens choosing consorts, falling in love, and being swept away with joy! (Gaia portal)

Faery Symbols

You will notice within these beautiful card images, painted by the faery and fantasy artist Selina Fenech, that there are recurring symbols.

Keys: Openings, entry points, codes, secrets to learn; knowledge

Ruins: Old ways, ancient paths, timeless places, lost lands, the faery world

Stones: Earth magicks

Ribbons: Wishes

Cobwebs: Communication, strands between people, generations, threads of love and memory, energetic cords

Wings: Faery wings are highly significant. A faery being with cicada wings, for example, has a different "temperament", different qualities to another faery who has, say, moth wings. All are beautiful, all are sacred. But look at the wings, and then learn more about the faery you are working with. The subtle differences are keys to knowledge.

Trees: Faeries often reside within trees, as their spirit. They tend to be tall, slender faeries, and are very beautiful, akin to the elvish beings. However, the smallest flower has her faery friend: of course, the daintier the flower, the tinier the caretaker. In large, old-growth forests, many powerful faeries dwell, and the power swells and is palpable!

Ears: Some are tiny and shell-like, others elongated and tapered at the ends such the classic pixie with pointed ears. Many faery beings have extraordinary (to us) hearing and are able to pick up a range of vibrations over vast distances. They can sense when something is "coming" long before those of us with human blood can. However, as many of us have faery blood, we too may have keen hearing and senses and may be able to pick up vibrations without actually being able to hear them. We are often extremely clairaudient – a classic faery trait!

Size: Faery-folk can grow to very tall heights, as the ones of the old forests and woods do, and they can be tiny, as those of the clovers are. They range in size from that of your little fingernail, to extraordinary, tall, glowing beings, known as the Shining Ones. All faeries glow; they are pure conductors of Source energy and as such, they shine. That is what they wish for you to do, too, and as you work with them more, you too will begin to glow. This will be spoken of as simply great health, but it is truly that the source within you is alight, and your own connection is alive again, and thus glowing and bright.

Form: Faeries must interact with other energies in order to be "seen", or to be energetically conceived of by humans. They are more ethereal than we, and must interact with our energy field to "materialize". This takes place when they sense a being they can truly trust, and when our eyes are open. If you cannot "see" them, take heart, as you will sense them; it is in your blood to do so! Belief does not need the sight of the physical form. Rely on your spirit eye, and all will be revealed! When you see green, golden, silver or bright glowing images at the corner of your eye, it is very likely a faery has just passed you by.

Bells: Awareness, signs, "alarms" and signals. Signs of the faeries' presence in your life, alerting you to their love and blessings. Avalonian faeries often ring silver bells attached to apple branches.

Cups: Holy Grail, filling up, being receptive, allowing others to give to you.

Hair: Faeries have very long hair, lustrous and thick, as they are so very ancient, and have been here since the mother, the earth, drew in her first breath. Their hair is another way of sensing and communicating. Their hair is "alive" and able to pick up and transmit signals.

Bare feet: Connection with the earth, connecting with leylines, drawing up energy through the feet chakras, heading in a true and authentic direction, protection, complete comfort with the planet.

Signs the Faeries are With You

You may hear rustling, glimpse a face within a tree, have a sweet puff of breath glance across your cheek, and even feel the faery kiss on your forehead! Bright lights may swiftly dance across a room, and orbs a-plenty will show up, cheekily stealing the limelight in your photos!

Faery chimes also may ring out, gently, or very very loudly at times! You may also hear bells, tinkling, and laughter. They are sweet-toothed, some of our faery friends, so do expect food to go missing, particularly honey. You may see sparkles, which is faery dust thrown into the air, feel light-headed, and your ears may ring as you enter a faery realm.

Faeries, in my experience, are not fearful of iron, as much as they are fearful of what we humans DO with iron – turn it into machines and weapons that hurt and destroy. Besides, gnomes are not at all fearful of iron – they are master metalworkers. So please, do not harm anything with iron. It is said that we should take flowers and cut plants with our hands, not with cruel iron shears – and always after seeking permission! And if you wish to see faeries more easily, one way is to smudge the pollen of a flower across your eyelids!

The Realms of Faery

...Princess Edane heard a voice singing on a May Eve like this, and followed half awake and half asleep, until she came into the Land of Faery, where nobody gets old and godly and grave, where nobody gets old and crafty and wise, where nobody gets old and bitter of tongue.

William Butler Yeats, *The Land of Heart's Desire*

There are all sorts of faeries, from country to country, and all sorts of faery lands. Here are only some:

*Welsh fae are called the Tylweth Teg, and the land they dwell in is called Tir Na Og.

*Irish fae are called, oftentimes, the Tuatha de Danaan, the shining ones, and collectively Sidhe. They live in the Underworld and are also embodied within the land and all her features (wells, waterways, mounds, rivers...)

*Avalon

*The Innerworld

*The Blessed Isles

*Faerylande

*The Manitou of the Algonquin people live within every flower, stone and droplet of water.

* Elfthame, or home of the elves

*Seelie Court. Often considered to be "good" faeries, they are helpful to humans and wish them to join with them in loving the planet.

*Unseelie Court. Not so fond of humans, as they feel we have been very harmful. Most of the Unseelie's have "given up" on us. 'Tis up to us to prove them wrong.

Dark Faery

Dark faery are oft-thought to be wicked and tricksy. Indeed they are tricksters, but mainly because of their disguise. You see, they wear the glamour of the dangerous ones as a protection. They are truly very soft and fragile souls, fearful for their survival amongst the urban ruins. They seek out and nurture every blade of grass that pushes through a cracked pavement; they find ways for natural waterways to break through and they guide the unicorn on dangerous missions at night. They are dark because they often work under cover of the night – and her darkness is soft. They are skittish and fearful at times, and though they are fearful of you, they will not harm you. In fact, the most harmful thing they can do is withdraw, as they have so often been told to do, by misguided folks who sometimes have thought they were casting out ghosts or dangerous spirits. The dark faery are like dark angels of the earth, and they are very necessary, and I for one, am truly grateful to them for the work they do.

Faery and Human Lovers

Faeries are indeed wild creatures, with their own laws and conventions. They are disciplined and adept, but they are spontaneous and free-spirited. When looked at from a conservative viewpoint they seem, and have seemed simply too much! They don't behave "nicely", they are not obedient nor are they compliant with paperwork and rules. They don't respect "authority" they do not give respect if someone is unworthy, no matter their wealth or station in life. They are cheeky, musical, artistic and while they certainly do "work" hard, they only do so at tasks for which they have true purpose and passion! (Many fashion designers clearly have faery blood!) Faeries do not see imaginative connection and expression as impractical and thus they are seen as unruly and unreliable.

And then of course, they adore true love. That is enough to make anyone a renegade!

Faery Spreads

More often than with other decks, you will find these cards to be tricksy. They are not difficult to use, it is simply that they retain some of that in-between magick of the faery realm. Your readings may take very little time, or you may lose hours, it would seem, gazing at these cards! Trance may steal upon you, so give yourself time and space when using them.

You may find cards jump out at you more often than with other decks you may have used. You may find that one being steps forward to speak with you over and over again, until the message is, well, received and gratefully accepted.

- Always make an offering before reading. If reading for another, ask them to make an offering.
- Read out of doors as much as possible.
- Always read with an odd number of cards.

These cards are a very accurate oracle, but they will tend to read your heart and energy, not your question, if it is not at the truth of the matter!

Questions to Ask Faeries

Faeries may not understand certain questions. For example, questions that come from the material aspects of ourselves or the ego may be outright ignored by faeries! They will find questions asking about whether you will win money or meet the right man very hard to comprehend.

They are very good with suggesting courses of healing, for all ailments, from chronic fatigue to heartache, to dis-ease to broken bones! They will assist with these issues and direct you to the true issues within a situation because they know it is spirit sadness and sickness that is creating the illness on the physical plane. They understand absolutely how the past impacts upon the present, so they will point, insistently, at what you may have thought is long over, so that you can root out a toxic form that could be creating illness or sadness and weariness now.

They are more interested in revealing to you the truth of magick, and thus, unless you have a question that is from your heart – and really, from your heart – they may override the question you seem to have asked, and read your heart, delivering the best answer anyway. They are true oracles; they see to the heart, and deliver what must be known for you to heal and return to true health. They can also give wonderful guidance regarding recovery from physical illness. Each of these cards holds a healing energetic pattern within, which will be "released" to you when you read the message and gaze upon the image.

When reading these cards, if you can possibly do it out of doors, that would be best! If not, have images and reminders of nature in your faery room. Setting up your altar outdoors will assist you in meeting and working with your faery oracle deck. The most auspicious times are at dusk and dawn, all the "between" times, as the faeries are able to live in the world between worlds. At Litha, Beltane and Samhain they are also most readily contacted. You may wish to do a reading each new moon, or full moon, to set up a regular energetic cycle with the faeries.

Places are important to the faeries. Where two streams meet in a forest, where a circle of trees grow together naturally, where a ring of mushrooms are, where butterflies have been seen – all these sorts of places will create a kind of magical world in which they will feel most ready to come to you. If this cannot be done outdoors, recreate such a place indoors, and ensure you have sprigs of thyme about, creating an energetic space which the faeries adore and know is safe for them.

What are Reversals?

You'll notice in your Faery Oracle guidebook, that for each card, there is a kind of message called a reversal or reversed meaning. The faeries asked for these to be included, so they could draw your attention strongly to issues, blocks, or areas where you may be somewhat "asleep". They are the faeries' way of waking you up to an important issue in your life. When you lay out your cards, you may find that one or more is upside down. That's because the faeries are working more deeply with you, and wish to draw your attention to a particular issue via a reversal.

Reversed messages do have a slightly different meaning. What's most important to know is that when this happens, the faeries want you to pay attention! The faeries, via reversals will indicate where and what the real blocks and unlearned lessons in your life are. Over time, your deck may even begin to have more reversals coming up. This is because as you connect more meaningfully with the faeries, you begin to really get to the heart of your issues.

When reversals come up, and they will come up, that means there's something going on, something that's calling out for attention and really needs your time and focus.

When you need to hear, see, get the message, the faeries will let you know! The faeries also wish you to know that reversals are not at all "negative". They simply intensify, or alter the upright meaning, and often indicate exactly where a deeper issue is. They are gifts, each and every time they occur in a reading, an invitation from the faeries asking us to gently awaken to conditioning and issues that we would benefit from becoming aware of, and then gently releasing.

Three Layouts for Faery Communication:

Seven-card Reading - The Faery Star

For this reading we will use the elvenstar, or septagram. This seven-pointed star is said to open a portal to the faeryworld. When I work with it, I draw it in the air before me, and it is through the center that the faeries can come to me, or that I am drawn to them.

Each of the seven points has a meaning for this type of journeying to and from the faery realm. Firstly, seven is a magical number, and sacred to many cultures and peoples. It symbolizes the seven chakras, the seven days of the week, the seven notes of the musical scale, the seven colors of the rainbow, the seven alchemical metals, the seven heavens. And seven is a number that is sacred to the faeries.

I often like to draw it with a wand, and as I do so, I see each point as having a meaning, much as you would if working with a five-pointed star. Then you can draw the image of the seven-pointed star out, until you get used to its appearance and can "see" it intuitively.

You can make this drawing a meditation and a drawing in of energy, too, by simply doing the following.

As I draw, for example, I visualize the points representing and "holding" the energy of: Earth, Air, Fire, Water, Spirit, Life, Magic.

And, just as a five-pointed star resembles the human form with arms and legs outstretched, the seven-pointed star resembles the faery form, alike to human, but with two more triangular forms and points representing their wings.

Begin by opening the circle and calling in the seven directions you will be working with for this rite. On your altar, light three green candles in the center. Place milk and honey on the altar as an offering. Place thyme there too.

Now, draw a seven-pointed star in one fluid motion with your wand, your athame (a short-handled witches' blade that is never used to cut anything on the earthly plane!) or your finger or wand.

Say out loud three times into the center of the faery portal you have just opened:

I call to thee, my faery guide
To allow me to see thee
Speak with thee
Know thee

Now, state your purpose, for example: "I ask you to come to me now, so that I may know more deeply who I am."

Allow your physical and etheric bodies to pour forth the motive behind this intent, that they may know you are pure of heart, one of the good folk yourself!

Now, see with your eyes or with your inner vision the center of this seven-pointed faery star begin to glow, and watch as through the center a faery being comes to you.

You may see lights, flickering or a soft glow. You may wish to close your eyes and use your inner vision completely. This is up to you.

Greet your faery friend and guide, and thank them for answering your call.

Ask their name.

Tell them why you wish to develop a relationship with the faeries.

Ask them to assist you in your quest to learn, and ask what you can do to help them.

Ask them three questions that you would like their insight on.

Shuffle the cards, and divide them into three piles with your non-dominant hand. Place the piles back together. Then, from the top, take the first seven cards.

And each can correspond to a direction. For example:

North – your body
East – your thoughts
South – your intent
West – your emotions
Above – your direction (Spirit)
Below – what you are hiding (Magic)
Within – the heart of the matter (Life)

The Faery Cross Reading

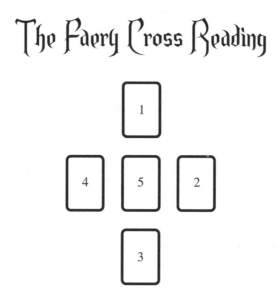

After shuffling and dividing the pack, lay five cards north, south, east and west. Lay one within.

- The north tells of your body, the material aspects of your question.
- The south tells of your intent and motivation.
- The east tells of your mind's thought patterns creating and shaping.
- The west tells of your emotions.
- And within is the heart of you, the soul stuff you are working with and integrating and transmuting through this "issue."

The Trinity Spread

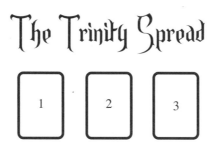

Another method is the very simple past, present future three-card spread. One to the left, one in the middle, one to the right. If you wish to know more about what is coming up, lay another card to the right. This represents what will happen over the next lunar cycle, or 29.5 days. If you wish to see further into your future, lay down another card to the right. Do this for as many moons as you wish to have information about. If you wish to have a "bigger" picture, lay down four cards to the right, and each of these represent three lunar months, or one year. You can then see the weaving of your story and what will be stepping forth for you to work with!

Always thank the faeries for their answers and ask them if you may talk with them again.

Some Closing Thoughts

After each reading, say farewell. Give thanks. Close the faery portal.

Remember to record your experiences and messages in your Book of Shadows and Light, best done before you reconnect completely with the "real" world.

Leave an offering, then ground yourself by placing both feet on the earth and raising your arms to the sky. Depart, clearing away all physical traces of your presence (ie pick up your rubbish!) but feel free to leave a crystal, seeds or flowers for the faeries.

May you have many, inspired and blessed readings. Above all, may the gentle hands of the faeries tend your wounds, awaken your bright spirit, and allow your true health and beauty to shine evermore.

Blessed be.

Card Interpretations

1. Three Graces

**Cooperative ventures with friends, Joy, Sharing,
New partnerships that are fun**

Every faery has a duty, a destiny and a realm where they are of service. Our duty is to assist you by example. By showing just how harmonious and joyful enterprise and sharing with others can be, you will soon be inspired in a cooperative venture. Your destiny is to find those beings with whom you can create joy and meaningful work aligned with your soul purpose. Your realm is currently to manifest this desire, to take it from a dream to the material and the earthly. We will help you make this dream a reality! For we are of the Springtime of the Soul, and we speak of a time of new growth and delight, harmonious enterprise and of finding just the right people to celebrate and work and create with. We are enjoying our association with each other, after long feeling lonely and isolated. When we discovered each other, our sense of fun and delight returned, and we knew that working on larger projects could be about joy, delight and harmony. There is no struggle or doubt in your new enterprise. You and your friends and partners will communicate smoothly and creatively. You will be compatible in your thoughts and feelings and expressions and skills, and all involved will understand the need for balance and fairness and fun. So, while we dance the world's magicks back into existence, you too will create magick in your new enterprise when you find the right people to partner with. As we represent the maiden aspect of the fae-goddess, this is a new enterprise. Please know that that the fresh, the new, the hopeful and the innocent is as vital and important as the established and the serious. We need this new energy you and your companions will create! Let us help you! We will guide you to new friendships and helpful new associates with whom you will get along well. It is important in our working lives to experience joy and harmony, and to have others to celebrate with is a gift indeed. We wish you to know that you will soon experience groups coming together to focus on a common emotional goal. People will reach out emotionally to one another. It speaks of a sense of community.

Divinatory Meanings

Finding like-minded souls to work with. A happy workplace. A new community is being birthed. Meeting new friends who feel like family. Overcoming trust issues with other people. Sharing, understanding and cooperation brings new opportunities. Joint business ventures. Growth of new friendships and relationships, bringing about play, delight and work that is in tune with your purpose and talents. Celebration of new beginnings. Dance and gentle movement. Synchronised fate of yourself with two or three other like-minded beings with similar outlooks, training, ideas and beliefs. New business ventures with friends. Amiable interactions with strangers.

Feeling happy and connected to female friendships. Feeling strong bonds with people although you have just met them. Creating a working magickal circle built on trust, delight, security and friendship. Rejoicing in femininity and feminine energies.

Reversed Meanings

You have had some hard experiences in terms of trusting others at work, feeling negative energies and experiencing toxic workplaces where the spirit was of competition and conquering. This has resulted in doubt and trust issues around finding people to spend time with. The Three Graces are assisting you in your quest to find like-minded magickal souls to play and to work with; and for you to know that you have the ability now to easily, effortlessly find these people, who will be like sisters to you. It is time to explore friendships, activate business plans with friends, and to overcome your mistrust of sharing with others. When the right souls are involved, all is safe and abundance is the natural result.

Solace
Return to nature, Tree wisdom, Natural remedies,
Flower Essences

2. Solace

Return to nature, Tree wisdom, Natural remedies, Flower essences

While you may be feeling fatigued and alone, the faeries advise that you do what they do when they feel down, saddened and in need of solace – return to the trees and to their wisdom. Trees and their energy speak to us, their voices slow and strong, tendrils of energy that caress and surround us. It is now time for you to find that tree, that forest, that old growth place where you can connect your energy with the energy of an ancient one – a tree who has seen so much, and who can ease you through this current time in which you are caught up in the problems that beset you. The tree will comfort you, lend you some of its energy, and soothe your hurts and ease your worries. You will emerge from this time healed, whole and happier. Peace is the result of seeking solace with these old and true friends. With every breath you draw in sitting with your tree, know you are breathing in their energy – their oxygen.

And with your every out breath, know that they are breathing in what you no longer need. Trees and human beings work beautifully together and the faeries want to help re-establish this relationship, for your own comfort and protection.

When you find your tree for healing, please ask its permission before sitting with it, then sit either within the tree, or with your back against the trunk. When you do so, a silvery, mist-like aura will surround you and the tree, and you may become aware of orbs and lights around you, perhaps seen only with the corner of your eye. This is how you know we are with you – for the faeries dwell with the trees, and we work together for the earth, our Mother. The only requirement we have is that by working with the trees for solace and healing, you will be able to comprehend how interconnected we all are, and how we need the old ones, the trees. By taking part in allowing them to clear your energy, you will work to help create safe places for these most powerful and wise of wizards – the trees.

Divinatory Meanings

Time to plant a tree. Feeling disconnected from nature. Time to garden and have plants and flowers around your home. Understand more about growth. Put down deep roots. Take time out to contemplate in a wild setting. Understand you are part of nature and of the earth. Starting to see and connect more with the natural world and with nature. Concern for the world's old-growth forests. Connection to the Celtic worship of trees and nature, and understanding that by doing so, you can connect with magick and the faeries more and more easily. If you dwell in a city, take time out for a park visit and a retreat into solitude (soul-itude and solace – soulace!) Connecting with bush and flower essences may be helpful at this time.

Reversed Meanings

You are spending so much time indoors; under light sources that cannot help you or heal you, that in fact are draining you and creating illness and anxieties within your body – and yet you are refusing to make time to connect with nature. This resistance is because you feel you "should" be able to do all you need to do on your own, with no assistance, but the faeries ask you to consider welcoming in the beautiful healing energy of the old and wise ones, the trees, for in this way, you will connect more strongly with the faery realm, and with powerful healing energies. Your resistance is only hurting you, and keeping you feeling victimised and sad! The faeries ask you again, to take yourself to a place, a park, a forest, a patch of green, where you can explore the healing available to you simply by merging with the energy of the old trees. You are of the earth. Denying that you are so will lead to feelings of disconnection from this planet. The faeries remind you that you were born out of her, just as they were, and that you are a beloved child of this beautiful planet, and to her natural realms you must look if you are to be whole, healed, and soothed from your worries, which are mere illusions. Let the faeries reach you through this natural world!

3. Riddle Fisher

Divination, Seeking out and finding answers

See how seriously this faery takes her mission? For her, it is a joy, even if she is earnest about it. And her quest is to find the missing piece of information you seek. But note where she searches…in the deep caverns of the ruins, in the ancient places of your emotions, of the past, of the memory, of your DNA, of the red line of ancestry that runs through you. This beautiful, calm and patient faery is searching through the waters of the deep caverns of the earth. The place where our truths can be hidden as more and more emotions pour forth, sometimes from the ego, hiding in their depths the truths and the answers we seek. This faery being is known as the riddle fisher, and her role is to search patiently, with intent and focus, on finding the answer to some of the most perplexing questions currently facing you. If you find yourself wanting answers, and not knowing where to start looking, this faery will assist you, by taking you into the depths of your unconscious mind, of your memories, both in this lifetime and in previous lifetimes, and in the memories of your family patterns. She will help you deeply search and calm down until the right answer is found. And for this she expects no reward, but you must honour your connection to your truths in order to connect to answers far more quickly. Faeries are also adept at finding material objects that are seemingly "missing", but which have often been moved deliberately by the fae in order to guide us to something that has been in our sights the entire time, but to which we have paid no attention at all. Never believe that something is lost. Because the faery beings will reveal its hiding place, and that will always lead you to something vital in understanding one of life's puzzles.

Divinatory Meanings

Time to seek out the help of the faery realm to find what is lost. Recovering lost memories. Past life readings and issues coming to the surface. Going through the emotional waters that are deep and knowing it is safe to do so. Feeling your feelings and knowing their wisdom. Searching for an answer. Water divining. Using pendulums and finding clues to quandries. Just as you are searching for answers, a faery is searching for your answers too – they love your puzzles, and will find things and answers and pieces of information for you that will put the current jigsaw into a meaningful picture for you. Come at this time – allow this faery to go on the search for you – you may not find the answers you were looking for, but you will find what is right for you!

Reversed Meanings

Not wanting to "go there"; avoiding the exploration of the emotional due to fear that it will hurt; a mistrust of therapy and processing your emotions, fear of finding answers to questions, denial of the unknown; ignoring psychic hunches and flashes; determination to keep moving in a straight line, rather than the circular path; an interest in alternative methods but no commitment to using them.

4. Storykeeper

Tell your story, Legacy, Write your wisdom

Live your life as if it is the greatest tale ever told! This does not mean to be intentionally dramatic, but it does mean to live imaginatively, boldly, magickally. Many people say they wish to write a book, but what they are saying, the faeries declare, is that they wish to record their life story, their wisdom, their experiences and the lessons they have learned. To have left this place having made a mark that has meaning. So, the Storykeeper is the faery being who comes to you now, showing you how she is writing down all the stories of all the peoples of the world, and yours too. It may be time to create a story for yourself, a rewriting if you like of the faery tale that is your life, and go beyond the "happy ending" where so many leave off. Find the inherent wisdom beneath the surface of the story. Which faery tale story have you been enacting? Which archetypes are coming up for you, and how can you take the pen into your own hands and create a story which resonates for you? The Storykeeper will write what you speak to her of, so it is time to seek the wisdom in your story, and change the patterns and twists that have repeated themselves and seem hackneyed and contrived. Carve out an original tale for yourself; create it from your dreams and adventures, and know that the Storykeeper will keep the record of your life on this earth alive for delivery to the Akashic record. Nothing you do is too trivial or small to be worthy of notice; all your tales and energies have an impact. Tell your story, but most of all, live your own story. Be original. And keep the Storykeeper supplied with fresh new material for her book of wisdom!

Divinatory Meanings

Time to tell of who you are. Share your story. Recognise that you are a record-keeper – what is it you wish to gift your ancestors with? Think of the generations to come and live your life as you would wish your story to be told. Bring what you dream of into reality on a daily basis. Tell the best story possible to yourself about your life; writing is therapeutic. Be original in your storytelling!

Reversed Meanings

Refusing to believe you can edit your experience and recreate the tale you are telling others; not understanding that the tale of your life is in your own hands; not recording the significant moments of your life; having intentions to write – not only to write for yourself but to communicate with others and leave a legacy, but not taking action. Feeling insignificant and wondering who you are to dare to contemplate writing and recording your story. Putting off quiet times for introspection; telling yourself you are no good at writing or storytelling. Wanting others to know who you are, but refusing to tell them about the great and secret moments of your life, not listening to others' stories, and feeling you do not know them. Feeling that you are not in touch with the wisdom-keepers, that ancient and deep knowledge is not for you. Underestimating the power of storytelling, of myth, fable and legend as the repositories of soul-truths.

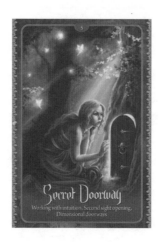

5. Secret Doorway

Working with intuition, Second sight opening, Dimensional doorways

This beautiful being is half-human, half-fae, and is rediscovering herself, and her ability to intuit the messages of nature – of all that is. She is an awakening being, who is undergoing a process of deep and real change based on her association with the fae, and her ability to finally understand that the trees and natural world are the keys to establishing communication with the fae. But she stands on the threshold of a world that seems ill-fitted to her; to understand and roam freely within, what can she do? Change her shape? Become smaller, like Alice in Wonderland? Truly, in order to reach the wonderment of faery, you must become "smaller". But that does not mean to become a reduced version of yourself. Rather, it means to approach them, or whatever situation is currently at hand, as a beginner, a walker in a new land, and to be humble and willing to learn. This threshold will see her

50

walk into another land, but she will still be able to walk in her own. See the light pouring through – through this humble doorway is en-LIGHT-enment. Meaning, more knowledge, understanding and the ability to communicate. She is peering through this doorway, through which light can shine into the darkening world of humans. A world that is only darkened by the thought forms that provide a kind of emotional pollution in our world. She is ready to step through, to allow her imagination's wisdom to lead her into new realms, and to accept the mystery of faery communication. They have much to share with her, and she is open to learning. Faeries circle about her now, rejoicing at this breakthrough, and she is breaking through her own fears of communicating with the faery beings, and has unlocked a doorway to another dimension. As a result, her life's work will start now, and she will find herself in the right place at the right time. As long as her relationship with nature remains pure and strong, so too will her relationship with the natural world. As this relationship deepens, her health and material wealth will also benefit in powerful ways, as the faeries love to see their own prosper and thrive, and take the messages back. She is a luminal being, an in-betweener, and will walk between worlds and in the three realms: of humans, of faery, of the afterlife (the Summerland).

Divinatory Meanings

Being able to see change ahead, but not knowing how to deal with it. Understanding that in order to learn something new, one must forget what one thinks one knows. Getting "down" to the level of others who you do not know. Receiving messages from nature. Understanding that wonderment is the natural process of change.

Reversed Meanings

You are receiving messages from the realm of faery, particularly tree spirits and beings, but you may be closing your eyes to these messages, refusing to hear them. Fearing these messages are not from a pure source as they do not feel celestial in origin. Feeling that light comes from above, rather than from within and underneath, and an unwillingness to be humble in the face of these messages. Humility, gratitude and an open heart will dissolve the dilemmas facing the seeker at present. Treating nature with love and respect, and some awe, too, will change so much for them. Above all, they need not overcomplicate, they must not judge. A possibility that judgement is rife, even if it is being called discernment. Mistrust of the world of this planet, and of its magickal beings. Refusing to be humble when faced with a change, a transition from one way of life to another.

6. Dark Moon

Maturation, Growing up, Introspection, Know thyself

This faery being seems shrouded in deep contemplation. Crooked in the cradle of a darkening moon from the northern hemisphere perspective, a dark air of regret swirls about her. This sad being represents the darkening – the time when we self-assess – and like her, grapple with understanding our response to a real test. She feels withdrawn, very young, very child-like, raw and untried. This is no failure of hers – she is facing the sadness that can lie within, asking the difficult questions. On her head curl the horns of the ram, showing she is a fiery being, one who has been brave and headstrong, and who for a time has stepped back to unfamiliar territory – that of the questioning of self. She is one of the few of her kind left, and her dilemma is that of feeling isolated and winnowed out, and of being treated unjustly. She faces a quiet kind of extinction, and knows that whatever she chooses to do now will determine her fate. And so she takes this time to ponder, and to sit, and to understand before acting. She is both masculine and feminine, her horns indicating many years of being on the earth, as they are mature, thick and heavily curling. She has survived on little over the years, and asked only to keep going. But now it seems she faces a real threat, and must take steps to not only survive herself, but to ensure that those like her continue on. From this dark time of deep contemplation, she will emerge and come out again into the world with strength, determination and knowledge. She will flourish again – but for now, it is the time of the dark night of the soul; and it is necessary and good, for of it wisdom will be born, and her kind will live wild and free once again.

Divinatory Meanings

Interestingly, this can be interpreted as a menopausal card for women, or one of seeming "bad news" bringing about change, as their moon times move to darkening. It is a time for understanding the frailties of the self and understanding the wisdom your years on this earth have taught you. Knowing that there is "nothing" that can be done at this time. Knowing that you need to understand where you are responsible for the current situation. Learning and taking ownership of responsibility will create freedom and new opportunities. Move through this and feel renewed, alive, and as though your own personal evolution is finally, finally underway. It will never be too late. The tests and the subsequent wisdom make this life here so worthwhile and will create your beautiful legacy for generations to come. You will rise up from this, as the phoenix is reborn from the ashes, just as the moon will wax and grow full once again. Have hope, but do spend time in contemplation.

Reversed Meanings

The reverse meaning is not so different to the upright meaning for this card, except that the person being read for may be under the illusion that this testing time is endless and they may be sliding into depression, mistakenly thinking that the current test is one which will endure forever. It *will* change. This is not forever. But it is for now. It is best at this time to actively embrace the introversion – sift through memories, explore your past, understand your patterns and identify the threats to your existence, happiness and true self flourishing. Alternatively, the person may be refusing any introspection or self-understanding at all, and insisting that action must be taken. Going for blame, rather than looking within the self. For now, pause. Stay still. Just for a time. And in that space, the shift will come, and flow and joy will return.

7. Faery Wishing Well

Manifestation, Expectations, Offerings

People have been making offerings at this faery wishing well for centuries, perhaps even millennia, but the gold they are leaving her is heavy with their expectations, so much so that her energy is drained as she struggles to undertake the granting of so many wishes. So she must carefully weigh each wish up, take it in her hands, and feel the energy. Those wishes that are for the highest good of all, that are made by people with open hearts, are granted, though that process can still take time.

Those who wish the faery to hurry up, those who are impatient, who keep questioning her and have a very fixed idea of how their wish must come about will find that their wish is rarely granted. It is not that she does not wish to, it is that she is tired and must have help. So, to make your wish come true, you must assist. Here is how you work your own magick to assist the faeries:

***Breathe not a word to a harsh and critical person about
your wish.**

*Nurture your wish with practical steps each day.

*Face your fears, and release them.

*Become ready for the wish to be granted.

You see, we can sometimes be granted our wish, often after a great deal of effort from the faeries, and yet we are not ready for that which we thought we wanted more than anything. So, our role is to trust, to surrender, to clear the way and do what needs to be done to be emotionally, spiritually and physically ready for the wish we have asked to be granted.

Also, we can send love and prayers and healing energy to the faeries of the wishing wells. It is significant that many of these sacred places were "exorcised" by members of the early church, and that the faeries were sometimes driven away. If there is a sacred spring near you, or a natural body of water, ask the faeries to come back in. Leave them an offering, without expecting anything in return. Then the faeries of these wishing places can return, and all of us, faery and human, all we magickal beings, will prosper and be joyful.

Build a faery shelter at the water's edge. A faery door will give them a portal through which to enter. 'Tis all in the intent with which you build.

Build a wishing well and ask a faery in. Do not burden them overmuch with wishes, instead, ask sincerely, from the heart, and then trust and know the wish will come through in perfect time. The faeries know more about timing that we!

Divinatory Meanings

This card is the card which demonstrates we have mastered the making of money in some respects. We have learnt of its ability to affect family, prestige and standing; we have allowed it to come into our life and we have seen some of the impact it can have. But have we learnt to allow it to flow like the waters of the well, and to trust that all our needs are divinely taken care of? This card, while showing us that creating with money is definitely something we are working at mastering, reminds us we may get caught up in that process and forget to an extent about the Source – which is ourselves and our connection with God. Is the magic circle of your coin ignited spiritually as well as materially? What is it that you are creating with your prosperity? Ponder these questions without judgement, and love being connected to both the Source and the outcome.

Reversed Meanings

Having no trust that your dreams will come true. Resisting taking steps to make your dreams come true. Wishing, but mistrusting, thus negating the faeries' work. There is the distinct possibility that you are feeling suddenly disconnected from your source, and lacking power over the flow of the money you have. Having created money is one aspect of prosperity training; another is the management and re-creation of this money. By re-creation, I mean that money has many lives. It is an energy that moves through many hands. Thus you may have made some money, but have lost it through ill-advised or emotional spending, including bingeing on items you could not afford, giving your money (your power) away to those who ask for it without honouring the lessons it can bring, for example, giving money away to partners or friends who will not pay you back. There is a real difficulty in terms of holding and recharging the energy of the abundance you have created, a lack of effort to honour what you have created. You need to go back to the energetic source of the prosperity you have created – the spiritual connection you have with the energetic fabric of the universe.

8. Cry For Nature

Mourning for something sacred which seems lost

You can see how saddened the faery-being here is and how she weeps for that which was cut down before its time had come. This old tree represents knowledge, and all that was once held sacred and secure, as it was once the home of this faery. Now, with its destruction and murder, she faces a time of deep grief. In your life too, there may be that which has caused you deep grief, when something that feels like a part of you has been taken away, well before its time has come. The grief you feel must be honoured, and expressed, and felt, for then healing can take place. There is no shame in weeping for that which seems to be lost. The tears are the water that brings new life, so do not feel you must hold back. This card indicates deep sadness and inner frustration on behalf of the questioner when confronted with the enslavement of the environment, animals, marine life and elemental life to "man's" needs. The effort to overcome these institutionalized brutalisations of our flora and fauna, of our earth, Gaia, can seem so very very great and can take so much energy. You may feel as you fight this good fight that you are barely making any progress at all, that you are restricted and thwarted and overwhelmed.

But the efforts you make will do more than change things – they will make you very strong, and you will be sending a ripple effect through our world, often without even knowing who you have inspired. Do not underestimate the impact you can have.

Divinatory Meanings

This is the card of the person who loves where they are – this planet. This person may be passionate about animals, nature, trees and protecting this earth. This person realizes they are as a child when faced with the ageless wisdom of all the creatures of this wonderful blue and green planet. Human wisdom is but one form. The being who has drawn this card is one with great elemental energy who can help rid the environment of toxic poisons and environmental pollutions. You will be passionately interested in helping the environment to be healed. In the same way, you are able to help heal toxic energy in places or in others – you may find you have a talent for clearing the karma of the environment.

This card is about the divine protection this magical planet enjoys from its special earth warriors. The person this card signifies has this earth warrior energy. The earth's spirit, in terms of the All who are attuned with this new earth energy – and we all have this capacity, regardless of age, religion, race, creed, family background and our issues – has the chance to change into a person of the new earth.

Reversed Meanings

In this card's case, the reversed position simply intensifies the upright position. The sadness may have fuelled a feeling of nihilism, one which many young people can experience, making them feel alienated, angry and can lead to self-harming activities. These young ones need to engage in meaningful activism to overcome their despair at the greed and lies that they can clearly sense all around them. They also need good food, plenty of physical activity, and must be cautious of being medicated out of their activism. If left without purpose, these young beings can find themselves lost, with a belief that all people are untrustworthy, greedy and materialistic. They must take action, become informed, be well, and raise their warrior voices to make meaningful changes that will help support this beautiful planet, and all of her beings.

9. Silver Sisters

Time to take protection from toxic thoughts and energy

Oh yes. They are looking at you. And they are not kind, these beautiful ones. But do not fear. 'Tis an indication that it truly is time. Time for you to clear, ground, balance, protect.

These beautiful faery-sisters seem so beautiful and glamorous: yet, sadly, they are here to warn you of energetic attacks through the form of harmful words and thoughts directed towards you. This does not create victimhood, but it is a call to understand that the malice of others does have an impact if we do not take the necessary steps to clear, ground, balance and protect ourselves each day from them, and others like them. There are those in the world who talk of us badly, who use their words in "jokes" and "jest", who say one thing to our face, and whisper another behind our backs. They do send out energetic poison in their gossip and nasty talk. And it can have an impact if your energetic health is not in peak condition. So, thank these nasty ones for reminding us to keep ourselves well! When the Silver Sisters turn up in your reading, it is not time to become fearful or paranoid, but to know that it is the nature of many people to ensure they feel better about themselves by talking and thinking badly of others. This is the true meaning of psychic attack. So, if they have visited you, you are being asked to create more energetic protection in your life, to seek out the barbs and arrows of jealousy and envy that may have taken root in your energy field, and to gently remove them. It is also time to be very mindful of your own words, and to clear gossip and negative thoughts about others from your mind and heart. Clairvoyant healers can often "see" where a thorn, barb or dagger has been thrown and they sometimes come from the least likely of places. The Silver Sisters remind us that appearances are not the truth, that sometimes, people behave in one manner, but beneath their appearance is much negativity. Trust your instincts on this one. When the Sisters turn up, you are being asked by the others in the fae-realm, who have also felt their sting, to learn to make your own environment, your own energy field, strong and bright, healthy and powerful. Because, as the Silver Sisters are here to remind you, there will always be those who snigger and laugh, who gossip and are cruel, and sometimes they are the ones who portray themselves as the most pure of them all.

The harmful energies or toxic auras, even psychic attacks, of others may be felt deeply by you at this moment. They may have penetrated your own energy field and become very difficult for you emotionally, leading to deep sadness, ill-temper, fearful feelings and a belief in your own unworthiness. As you separate out your own beliefs, your own issues, from those projected onto you by fearful family, acquaintances or co-workers, give thanks for this insight, and cut your cords to others each day. If this card turns up for you in a reading, it is utterly vital for you to learn to discern between what is your stuff, and what has nothing to do with you. Give thanks when others teach you this lesson.

Divinatory Meanings

It is time to approach your energy work in a disciplined way each day, until it becomes second nature. When learning the lesson of this card, it can be a short step away to feel victimized, harassed or picked on. Take all necessary measures within the law and the bounds of what you understand to be right to protect yourself, along with moving through an attack without being touched because you have strong protection and good psychic health supported through practice and discipline. You are sensitive, and because of that, you must trust your instincts and your ability to discern what is truly taking place. Lies and hurtful things are possibly being said. Do not retaliate. Take action on your own self. You will not be hurt when you realize that the weapons of attack have nothing to do with you personally, even if you are being attacked personally. You are not other people's ideas about you. Do not become their lie by responding as if you are. Clear, ground, balance and protect yourself.

Reversed Meanings

Refusing to believe that people can be cruel. Not understanding or acknowledging the impact of harmful words, thoughts, behaviour directed towards you. Not taking the necessary steps to clear, ground, balance and protect yourself. Feeling you should be "tough" and able to "take it." Critical of yourself for being "too sensitive." Inadequate energetic protection and disciplines in place to cope with the energy you are currently experiencing.

Taking on other people's opinions and experiencing a lack of self-definition — meaning you are easily influenced against your higher self's better judgement. A tendency to believe the criticism of others, no matter how little it resonates with you on a soul level. Taking on other's beliefs as your own. Feeling like a bad person when you are truly a perfect, innocent and loving child of All.

Search your heart for times when you have indulged in harmful gossip, and remove this from your life. Make a commitment to not read gossip magazines or watch programs that revel in malice, and to not speak ill of others, even of those who seemingly have hurt us.

10. The Unicorn and the Maiden

Communication with unicorn, Purification,
Undercover action

In this beautiful card, the sacred Unicorn and the magickal faery-maiden are preparing for a mission. The maiden lives in the "world", the real world, as we say, that we inhabit day to day. There she does undercover work on behalf of all that is magickal, true, and soul-ful. Her ally, the Unicorn, is to go to the etheric places, and share her work with the creatures too long in hiding, and ask them to come forward and let themselves be known again. Together they are discussing what must be done next. The Unicorn knows this information will be safe with the maiden, and the maiden knows too that she is safe with this magickal creature – but they also know that there are those who would hunt down the Unicorn for its marvelous knowledge, its magicks, its alicorn with its healing properties, and the mystic ruby that lies beneath its brow, giving those who possess it the power to see into the hearts of those around them and know their true intent.

But together, they know they can do their work. They meet in the in-between places, out of sight – in your dreams, visions, meditations and pathworkings. But it is her job to take the information back, and to translate it into material form. It is in this way that purifying and detoxifyng vast areas can take place. They both work for peace, and they both are able to see right into the hearts of those around them.

Among their many skills, unicorns have the ability to create peace, even when confronted by great aggression. (One stayed famed warlord Genghis Khan's hand, turning him back from battle and choosing peaceful settlement of differences.)

Unicorns also bring about the power of the written word. They communicate the tale that needs to be told. This holds true for artists too, as the original language the Unicorn developed was pictorial, so they are behind many film projects, novels, television series and visual arts and collage, most especially. If this card has appeared to you, and you are embarking on a creative project, simply ask for the help and guidance of the Unicorn, who will fill you with inspiration and help you through any block you may be having regarding writing.

The unicorn's horn emanates from the center of his brow, the region in which his (and our) third eye and third eye chakra are located. The third eye contains our capacity for intuition, for psychic abilities, for clairvoyance and for communion and communication between worlds. When this card shows up for you, the messages you are receiving are very likely to be reaching you through that point. We can use our intent, our energetic power, emanating from that point too, to pray over our water, to seek out peaceful solutions, and to keep precious, rare and sacred beings safe from harsh and toxic environments.

If the Unicorn and the maiden appear to you in a reading, you are being reconnected with your magical self, with your own maiden, your own pure, wild qualities. Gentle and free, fierce and beloved – as is the magical creature, the beloved Unicorn.

Divinatory Meanings

The Unicorn is a symbol of ancient magicks rising, and purification of the earth and the etheric realms taking place. The maiden and the Unicorn standing together indicate that you are receiving communications about detoxifying, clearing your environment, following your life path, and being a peaceful activist for change! The doors between worlds, for you, are growing wider and wider. More and more is coming through for you. Please know that you have a purpose, which is in the moment now, to help the environment. You are a peaceful being, sensitive and yet so very strong and powerful. Keep some of your works secret; do not try to attract attention. The new children, who are becoming adults now, are aided in their life purpose by the Unicorn. It is time to protect and help something precious and threatened, to survive. Bless your food and water to ingest healing Unicorn energy.

Reversed Meanings

Misunderstanding and underestimating your own power to bring about peaceful solutions to a difficult challenge. Feeling alone and unsafe; unsure of whether your visions are authentic. Feeling deluded and confused by visions and psychic communications. Unsure of the purity of the source you are receiving your communications from. Feeling hunted and as though you must hide away to be yourself, and to be safe. Headaches in the third eye region. Psychic information flooding in in apparent disorder. Not following through with your life's purpose of creativity. Not taking up pen and paper to write the letter that can contribute to a peaceful world. Eating and drinking food and fluid sources that may have impure origins or contaminants. Food poisoning, preservatives, heavy metals and toxins in food and water need to be replaced and purified.

11. Barnubus and the Prince

Adventures, Discovery, Travel, Meeting destiny

The journey, explorer, seeker, wanderer, hero. For your dreams to come true, you must take action and get out of your comfort zone! Then you will be in the right place, at the right time.

In this strong and powerful card of seeking out your soulmate, the prince is actively in search of his true love. He knows she will not be a "missing" part of him, he does not seek to find another just like him, only in female form. He will know, though, when he finds his true love, because the frog will sing his song when she is reached. You see, in the lore of the frog, their voice heralds a downpour, the refreshing rain quenching the thirst of the dry earth. For Barnabus, a seeker and prince on a quest, his dream is about to be realised. So, when you receive this card in your reading, you know that your quest and your search is going to create new opportunities, and there will be a successful "end" to the search. You will find what you seek, and so much more. Listen for the song of the natural world. When you hear it, that is when you know your wish has been granted. You need to quest, to see your search as a journey, an adventure, and even travel to go where you are being guided to bring about the realisation of a dream. The way to find love, adventure, gifts and mystery is to be brave, and go, finally, on that quest!

Divinatory Meanings

A dream, a vocation, success, or purposeful activity is reaching out for you, just as you have reached out for it. Use the power of your voice to call out for it. Let the world and the natural world know that you wish for them to deliver. Seeking out a mate. Actively searching for a soul mate, searching for you… synchronicity. In order for you to be in alignment with your dream, for your dream to dream you, you must be walking the right path, and be in the right place at the right time. So this card reminds you that staying in your present comfort zone will not bring about that which in your heart you yearn for – you must become active, and create. It also reminds you that travel and adventure can bring about soul growth that will let your song grow stronger - and it is in this way that your soul kind can find you. Have no fear. The drought will be broken. But you must be an adventurer! Your tears will cleanse the way. You will change several times throughout this lifetime; reincarnating within the one life. You do not need to "die" to go home or be with the one you love. What kind of transportation do you use? It may be time for a re-think.

Reversed Meanings

Refusal to move, to seek out, and to be courageous. Staying at home, being introverted even when you know the time to extend yourself is here. Refusing to actively engage in creating what it is you wish for. Anti-heroic stance. Feeling cynical and unmotivated about love. Telling yourself that travel and movement is not necessary for you, that you cannot, and becoming adept at excuses to justify your status. The refuge of the broken hearted is to say "love does not exist" and that "all men are bad". Time to open up to the potential partners in your life, and see them at a soul level.

12. Gossamer Princess

Communication, Relationship work to be done

This beautiful young faery maiden sits atop a delicate spider's web, one that is literally "hanging by a thread." She is making a decision, whether to reweave the strands that support her at present, or whether to move on and recreate her web elsewhere. This card can show up in your life when you are reaching a point in a situation or relationship where the strands need to be rewoven or changed. For, just as a spider does each morning, all our relationships and connections need this regular tending. It would seem that there has been some neglect of important strands in your life, and you are at a point where you are wondering whether to repair or to move on. There may have been some breakdowns in communication: not having heard from a friend, speaking less with family members or not paying attention to the small things that bind us together. Though the strands seem so delicate and gossamer thin, remember that they are strong indeed. When spider spins, her strands can withstand wind and rain, storms and damage, ice and burning sun. All it takes is the gentle reweaving, each day, for relationships and connections of great strength to endure. In that tending, all things will be recreated, and perhaps in that recreation they will be changed, and be even better and stronger than before.

Divinatory Meanings

Because it is communication between yourself and others at the heart of this card, you may be experiencing communication difficulties: your phones may be down, the web may be playing up, your email or other sources of technology may need some repair work. Relationships might be fraught with trivial misunderstandings, leading to falling outs that are unworthy of both parties. Consider spending time with people you have not seen for some time and know that whatever you decide, it is worth spending just a little time to assess the relationship's meaning to you. Connect with others to feel less isolated; share your creations and your thoughts and feelings. The need to talk through issues affecting yourself and others. Sharing your truth with respect. Waiting for another to make the first move in communications. The web of family, of life, between friends and species. Interrelationships. There is always the possibility to recreate the web. Endings and gentle separations. End of one part of life, changing from one stage to another. Young women. Coming into the initiation stage.

Reversed Meanings

Reversed, this card can relate to the etheric cords that bind you, keeping you from seeking and pursuing your life purpose. This card also indicates that some of your relationships in the world are being maintained only because you fear that if you sever the ties you have, you could fall. There is a real sense of defining who you are through your relationships, both personal, and professional.It may be time to gently allow some strands of your web to dissolve and to build again elsewhere. It could be time to change your technology and to take some time out to think on your own for a while. If you decide to retain the relationships, know that there will be a delicate repair job ahead of you. Reluctance to rebuild after apparent change and to take responsibility for your part of the web, your part of the relationship. Waiting for another to "fix" things. Hesitation. Lacking confidence in your ability to bring about change. Underestimating your strength and ability to bring about positive change. Feeling it may be best to allow some parts of your life to come to a gentle end.

13. Catch Me

Trust, Surrender, Leap of faith into the unknown

This faery-woman has no discernible wings: yet without them, she still knows she will fly. She is trusting and moving forward, and although all around her are panicking, and wanting her to stay where it seems to be safe, she has faith, and she will be supported.

This card denotes the creation of the wise, surrendered self, often birthed through some kind of crisis. She is the newly created being, and her energy is innocent, unworldly, trusting and therefore extremely powerful, potent and magickal.

This being is completely trusting. She is fully focussed on listening to and following her inner voice. She has no worldly protection, her arms are outstretched, and she shows no fear as she walks off the edge. Her self-belief in this remarkable situation is not pride, for she is focussed on going ahead. This is the greatest leap into the unknown – the Leap of Faith we so often speak of.

She may seem to have nothing but faith, but in truth her repository of instinctual knowledge is held within her magickal, miraculous self. The storm clouds have gathered about her, but she is unafraid – or rather, has gone past fear, and into acceptance. She knows that what will be, will be, and that to walk forward is to create an immense possibility of miraculous healing, and a profound shift. She is the divine embodiment of Trust.

She represents all who take great chances, which in turn allow us to connect with our spirituality. 'Catch Me' embodies the lesson of faith in our own soul renewal. This card symbolises the courageous leap of faith, the trust in intuition. We have no obvious means of survival, and yet we know we will, and we will walk into our future, come what may.

Divinatory Meanings

It is time to take a chance that others may see as very risky. But it is time, for if not now, when? On a mundane level this beautiful card can indicate a person who takes what others may judge to be almost crazy risks. It may represent a person leaving a safe job, entering a new relationship wholeheartedly, making a move in life without having examined all the consequences. But she is not someone who is foolhardy. She sees no crazy risk because she is only acting in faith that the path of courage and trust is the only path she can take. When she acts out of inner guidance, there is nothing to fear, and thus fears are not realised. Her feet, strong and bare, will leave the safety zone, and the healing path will be carried forward with her into the unknown adventure. She has transcended.

Reversed Meanings

Experience is our teacher, but we must not live energetically in the past. To do so is to risk never changing, and change is life itself. This faery is taking what seems to be a great "risk" and doing "the impossible". So if this card turns up in a spread reversed, it could well signify that you need to trust your inner voice more. You need to walk towards your own precipice, your own impossible feat, and take a chance. What could that be? Leaving a relationship? Knowing you will get through a tough situation? Finding your voice and speaking your truth? Believing in your abilities? The being in this card may not have wings, but she has faith, and such trust. What are you placing the power of your belief in? Is your belief supporting you or hurting you? What innate aspect of your wisdom do you need to re-connect with? Ask for help and assistance in facing your fears and walk into the future without having a guarantee. There are no guarantees. There is only the magickal power of trust, faith and surrender. And you will be uplifted and safe, as long as you focus on staying out of fear.

14. Light the Darkness

Ancestors, Ancestral line, Generational shift

A tiny, bright, childlike faery straddles the grizzled head of a faery-elder. What can this mean? In faery lore, the head is particularly significant. It is in the head that inspiration, fire and power are said to reside. The faery told the ancient Celts of this secret, and the Celts then venerated and collected the heads of the heroes slain, which often were said to live long after the "body" had passed away. And this small bright faery is hearing of all the wisdom this old being has. He is sharing, telling and communicating, and while she may seem playful, she is attending to his every word, and she will remember for generations to come. You see, faery do not live forever, though they live very long lives, a great deal longer than any humans do, even the ones with human blood. However, they do fade away, and the small faery being atop the head of the old one will ensure the knowledge continues on.

On another level, the small brightness of the faery represents Inspiration, the muse, the fire in the head which we speak of in Celtic shamanism. It is when we feel and see and know that connection to all that is, when we are afire with inspiration and ideas that flow to us and from us and within us, that we are restored to our true self. This beautiful ancient being whose light is fading, is passing on this wisdom into the keeping of the young and often underestimated.

Divinatory Meanings

Listen to elders. Find a playful, wise elder from whom you can learn. Seek out relatives and ancestor wisdom. Search through your family tree for evidence of the magicks within you; they are there. Old wise ones have messages for you and you can learn much from them. Allow them to pass on their wisdom to you so a living tradition continues. Understand that you come from a long line of wise ones and connect with those elders. A chance encounter with an older person gives you much to think about. You will learn a great deal at this time if you connect with older people. Do not be afraid of growing older. You will never die, your light will be passed on, and your soul-spark will return to Source, to star-fire, to be renewed again, only as you agree to.

Reversed Meanings

Only sticking to people your own age. Knowing little about your older relatives. Mistrusting people who are older. Stereotypical thinking and beliefs about older people. Needing to connect with other older people but feeling cut off from them, feeling they are unlike you. Believing that the generation gap is too wide to be bridged or that bloodlines don't matter. Denying your DNA. Wanting to cut yourself off from your family of origin, and their history and traditions.

15. Stolen in Her Sleep

Unaware, Unconscious, Unawakened

The beautiful being in this card represents what we all know we have been at some time in our life – we have been a sleeper, unawakened to our own experiences. We have not been present, awake, or even aware of what has been happening. And this beautiful being is so deeply enchanted and enspelled by conditioned thinking, by the "sleep" of her untested beliefs, that the only answer for her now is to go deep into the underworld, where she will be reconnected with the earth and reborn. But for now, she is as one slumbering through her life, in fear, never in the present moment. She is so stuck, so set in the ways of fear and programming, that it is time for the powers of the deep elementals, the earth, to take her in so she can be transformed. And, just as she resembles beauty, she is indeed asleep to her own light, her own freedom, and her own blessings. And it is time for her to be transformed. Be not afraid for her, for the gnomes of the earth element will take her in, care for her, and then return her safely home, transformed. She will awaken once again and she will realise that it has been long since she was in the presence of Life and offered up thanks for all she has been given. She will see as though she has never seen before, hear birdsong clearly and with understanding. She will feel intensely and know that it is safe to do so. And with her rebirth will come a fresh, new beginning, from her heart, extending outwards into the world. This going beneath is not to be feared, for it is a time of healing and reawakening to her true self.

It is not as it seems – she is not being stolen from her slumber – she is being taken from a place of sleeping to who she is, to a place where she will be awakened and return with the full-consciousness of all that she is. And that is a gift indeed.

Divinatory Meanings

Unable to remember dreams. Feeling cut off from psychic abilities. Unsure of whether the path you are drawn to follow is safe. Feeling scared that you may be entering a dark realm. Wishing to go "home" and to ascend before you have done the deep work on the self. If this card has come to you it is time to go deep within, to go into the earth and to understand that material transformation is spiritual. It is then that your gifts will be fully awakened.

Reversed Meanings

A refusal to allow yourself to undergo the deep rites of the consciousness which we need to undergo in order to awaken. A fear of going deep within, of discovering aspects of yourself that you may find unattractive. Resisting the chance to wake up to what this lifetime is truly all about. Staying in the routine. Being "dulled and deadened" by believing your life is that of meaningless repetition. It is time to entrust that going deep within will assist you and that you will be safe. Fearing that going within is evil, scary, out of the realms you have learned. A fear of religious and spiritual processes and traditions and new thoughts that are outside the mainstream. A mistrust of the grounded, connected quality that the body has. A feeling that the physical is unspiritual.

16. Her Special Place

Find your own safe space – inside and out

Sanctuary, solitude and an oasis in which to hear the sound of your own heartbeat. That's what this beautiful faery wants you to find. A sweet and safe place in which you make time for yourself. And she knows that in order to know our own truth we need that place where we can safely be on our own, to revel, dream, and be. We need this safe space more often than we think – and for you, you need it now! Therefore, she asks you to develop this space for yourself, so within it you can just…be. There are ways for you to create this sacred haven for yourself. This faery being is sharing hers with you, so that you can feel the peace and tranquillity and safety she experiences when she has her times there. Just as she has found a lily pad island where she can hide away, drift, and just feel safe and in solitude, so too can you create and nurture that space in the world, and that space inside of yourself. Consider simply spending time alone in nature or being with friends who are soothing and accepting, yet with whom you can be totally yourself. Go within and get to know who you are. Realize that you are a sensitive, sacred being who deserves self-nurturing. Please take time out and renew your sacred self.

Divinatory Meanings

Her Special Place can signal a need for solitude and quiet, a break from busy-ness, strife, and stress. Find the way in which you respond with healing and love and give those things to yourself. Take a break from hearing about disasters and create an oasis where only some can enter, and only at your invitation. This card can signal a need for a haven, a sanctuary, where you can commune with your own emotions and have some time out that will refresh and restore you when you re-enter the world. This is a time of introversion, not of sadness, but of turning towards the oasis, sanctuary, and the peace that exists within. We are all born with this place within us; it is simply that we sometimes forget, or lose our connection with it.

Drawing this card could signify that it is time to put energy into creating your own special place: a room or home, or a space to work where you feel safe, creative and without judgement. This card can also signify that you are healing from health and emotional issues because you have worked hard on creating a physical space in which you are treated with love and respect – by yourself, firstly, and by others. This beautiful faery's appearance could also signal a remission in health issues. Renewal and healing may be as simple as finding a quiet place near a still body of water and doing what you most love. Alternatively be sure to follow the "as within, so without" creed – create peace inside and that external peaceful place must manifest. So, through meditation and the nurturing of the inner sanctuary, the external one shall appear.

Reversed Meanings

No personal space at present. Feeling space is invaded. Wanting to heal, but unable to create or contemplate taking the time out to do so. You may be undergoing life changing experiences yet refusing to change your life. There is likely to be an avoidance of inner issues, a failure to take time to understand your own part in your life lessons. Invalidating the healing energy of nature and of personal space; the "I cannot meditate" mindset. Relaxation response ineffective and being drowned out by the need to press forward without reflection. No time taken to process the meaning of the journey. An imbalanced focus on destination and goals at the expense of the wisdom and growth of the journey. You may be finding yourself bored with your own company, or "doing nothing". Feeling that you have no safe space that you can go for rest and respite. A sense of not truly having a home that is yours.

17. Acorn's Invitation

Touch, Exchange, Connection

This beautiful faery man is inviting you to touch the world, to enter into a somatic relationship with the world around and within you. To experience the vitality of the life force that exists in everything, including you, and including your body, with which you may have a conflicted relationship. The faeries know that your body is a beautiful sacred expression of the spirit and an essential part of the self. They teach that when we reach out and touch, not only do we connect with another, but we are touched in return. Thus through the act of physical communion we are touched, held and nurtured. It cannot be otherwise.

The impact of touch is so underestimated, but this faery man wishes to remind you that without touch, you can become sad, depressed, unwell and your immune system weakens. The touch of the faeries is also touch – slightly different to that of human on human, but it is a physical and energetic exchange nonetheless. While you are alive in your current form, this faery wants you to know that you must touch and be touched to be whole. Physicality is your friend. Hug, hold hands, rub a back, get or give a massage, rub feet and connect. Allow a butterfly to alight on your finger. Pat a dog. Stroke a cat. Look into someone's eyes while you sit with knees touching. For this touching is healing, and touch has the ability to uplift us, comfort us, soothe us, cure us, and make us vibrate with bliss.

Touching is an absolutely mutual act. As we touch, we are touched in return; therefore it is a way of exchanging energy. There is no way to touch another without being touched in return, and that is why experiencing the physical without guilt, judgement, fear and shame is an experience of the faery realm, one which they can teach us so much about.

The faeries teach us that the world of the earth, the material world, is – when created consciously and with respect – a precious gift of the spirit. We have the right to honour and experience that gift. Touch, and the ecstasy that can come from your physicality, is a blessing the fae wish to remind you of. Explore touch and sensuality, and give and receive. Allow yourself to experience your body as a gift of delight, health, friendship and communion. You will then activate healthy, mutually enriching relationships.

Divinatory Meanings

This card also represents a beautiful man: physically appealing, earthy in nature, well in body, healthy in sexual appetite, who has a strong association with the archetype of Robin Hood or Robin Goodfellow. He has something of the faun or satyr or Pan about him, and while he is a man, truly, he is also there to help his woman by loving and honouring her physicality. A unique aspect of the faery realm is that it honours both the Goddess and the God.

Faeries teach us to be vital, to be healthy, and that part of this is to glory in our physical selves and our physical desires. This faery man is not talking about a kind of base physical gratification, a filling up of a void, an appetite sated. He is speaking of true, communal, healing, loving touch. As his fingers caress the earth, so he respects and loves the woman, the feminine, the mother, the crone, the maiden. He reminds us that when we touch something, we are in communion with it. We are at one with it. Touch is an energy communion, and an exchange between two or more people or beings. No one can touch and be left unchanged. When we touch with faery fingers, super sensitive and fully aware and conscious, we experience the sublime, and make better choices about who we touch – and who touches us - and why. Massage. Love-making. Earthy sensuality. Touch therapies.

Reversed Meanings

Feeling untouched, craving physical contact, sensuality. Starved for physical attention. Mistrust, fear of physicality. A dislike of the touch of others. Feeling uncertain about who to touch, when to touch them, how to touch them. Hesitating in allowing yourself to experience the visual pleasure of desire. Finding the material "unspiritual." Resentment of the body. A feeling that touch and physical satisfaction is unspiritual.

18. Scared to Fly

The right moment, Sensing out the right timing

New life is coming, spring is stirring, the sap is rising through the barren branch onto which she clings, and this faery is longing to let go and fly forth to tell all that spring has come at last! But she cannot until she feels the life force swell irreversibly, and though she can feel it coming, the time is not quite right yet.

This is the card that indicates it is almost time and that you must be ready for when the time is right. The faery being in this beautiful card is awaiting the energetic sign, and holding on until magick itself signals to her it is time to take flight. Though she seems a small and lonesome figure, she can and will fly and alert all to the coming of the green time, of leaf bud. But for the time being, the bare tree seems like the only available shelter in this landscape – and it is, if you take the limited view. But who knows what lies beyond? When the right time comes, her flight will activate change, and bring leaf bud, and new life to all. If she times this right, all will be well, and the seasons will continue their turning.

One beautiful aspect is that she is alone in this timing. She must rely on her faery-sensitive senses, and heed no voice but her own and that of the natural world. She has direct communication with the planet and when the time is right, the breeze too will gather force and support her in sending her work and message out into the world.

This card is about suspending activity and being in the moment – awaiting the right moment, knowing that when you are in that flow, all will unfold perfectly. Just by being where we are we may understand so much of where we have been, and where we will go – and we can certainly refine what it is that we want, value and desire.

Think of the chrysalis, hanging, seemingly static from a branch, fragile and mysterious. It "does" nothing but become itself. Become who you are by being in this chrysalis-like state, by awaiting the right moment to emerge and share, just like this faery. Transformation is inner before it is manifested outwardly into the world. You must wait for the time to be right.

Simply by doing this you will affect change. Your energy itself will change the situation – and your reaction is an indication of great wisdom. It is hard not to react, or to project our fears onto others, to blame and take everything personally. Very hard! Let us not underestimate the challenge of this card. To wait for the right time (which is of course choosing to act with self-mastery) is not passive – it requires rethinking and challenging the outmoded conditioning that claims that only by rushing in can we activate our own impact and energy within a situation.

The wisdom (very very challenging wisdom) you are being required to show, demonstrate, learn and teach is unlike that which the world generally recognizes and respects – it is the strength, the power of endurance and seeming inaction, of waiting. Internally, there is great pressure to be active, external, creating change. But the energy of this card is inner mastery through demonstrating patience.

On a spiritual level this can indicate the lesson of Surrender. Once you understand the precious and timeless nature of being, and the fact that time is not linear, you will move forward and into your strength and purpose in divine right timing. The faery and nature will show you, with a clear and natural sign of "it is time."

Divinatory Meanings

It is time to sense the atmosphere and wait for the right moment. It is not time to go when you are "told" by another, but when you know you are ready. It may look like hanging on or fear to others, but in fact you need just a little more to support you, and then you can fly high. It is truly about synching into lunar cycles and finding the right time for this venture to take flight. When planning this step, be sure to do it at the right time, when the moon, the energies and nature herself supports moving forward. Learn more about the natural festivals and the lunar cycles and plan your step accordingly. Do not rush. Know that good things do take time and that slowly can indeed be a worthy way to work. Rushing can create dilemmas, so sense out what is right for you and get ready to fly higher than ever before!

Reversed Meanings

Wanting to rush the results. Unsure of whether doing nothing is good enough. Eager to "get on with things". Impatient for your time to come. Unwilling to wait for the energy to be right for you to move forward again. Seeing stasis as "nothingness". Unwillingness to let events unravel. A lack of faith and belief in divine right time. Needing to see the evidence of your own impact on a situation that may not require that particular kind of involvement from you. Change for change's sake. Forcing an issue before its time.

19. Faery Tales

Letting go, Detachment, Moving on

This is the card of seeming cruelty. How can you or another leave anyone who loves them and needs them so? But the truth is, it is time to detach and set yourself, or another free, even though it may seem you are abandoning them to a kind of death without you. This is not the truth. The truth is that you must let go of anything that is currently suffocating, restricting or dragging at you, and while this is the most difficult thing for you to do, do it you must. It will be very hard and there is a chance you will face a great deal of guilt. Others may find you cold or fail to understand how you can leave someone so devoted to you. While you have had terrific experiences and wonderful connections, with these have come responsibilities that have accumulated to the point where you are identifying with them so closely that you no longer feel free. Please, one by one, take these burdens – anything that feels heavy, whose energy does not come from love but from need, any demands and expectations that no longer meet your needs, and gently let them go! There is no rejection in this gesture: it is simply a time to re-establish your own personal boundaries. You may even be carrying burdens that rightly belong to other people – please, release these NOW. By releasing them, you can call on your deity, angels, elementals of the universe to send these unwanted and unnecessary illusions we call responsibilities to heaven. The emotional freedom, lightness and joy will then pour into you. Without this kind of clearing, you may well feel you are carrying too much, and are unable to see the path ahead of you. This card can often come up when there are issues of addiction: overeating, unhealthful weight on the body, emotional issues from the past, guilt, a feeling of unworthiness; all loading you up and causing you to take tiny, painful steps on your journey.

This is a sign from the Universe that by releasing these burdens you are being brought closer to who you really are – a divine child of light. As you do this releasing, tiny streamer-like wings will sprout from your back and the beginnings of the sweet and tender freedoms that are your birthright will make themselves known to you. You are now free to love and care for others more effectively, as you will be acting out of love, not forcing yourself. Blessed be, reborn one. The time has come to let go and move on.

Divinatory Meanings

You will see miracles take place. Remember we teach others how to treat us, and you have similarly taught yourself what you feel you are worth, and taught others to rely too heavily on you. However, it is not too late to change. You are not refusing to save a life, though that is how it looks to your own critical self, and perhaps to some others. At the moment, you feel your worth is derived entirely from being of service to others, even when you feel you can no longer go on. You are currently a one-person rescue squad, but until you help yourself to be free of such expectations, you will never be free enough to be of help to others. Resentment, guilt and anger can leak into the "service" you are providing. Please contemplate a fresh way of communicating and begin to love yourself and give yourself regular work breaks and time out. When you can begin to respect your contribution, others will too. Please set them all a loving, inspiring example.

Reversed Meanings

Feeling that "good people" do not leave or change when others need them. Feeling suffocated by the need of others. Needy people who are draining energy without permission. Hanging and clinging on to all your "responsibilities". Working harder and more doggedly than any other person expects you to. Staying beyond a healthy relationship. Refusing to leave because you believe that would make you a "bad" person. Refusal to clean out old issues, situations and people. A victim mentality that keeps you in martyr mode. Giving away your power and an extreme fear of shining your light. You must lovingly release these beliefs and attitudes one by one and replace each belief. Know that your personal freedom is an innate truth of who you are, not something that needs to be struggled for. You must set yourself free.

20. The Littlest Faery

Appreciate the beauty and value of the exquisite and small

Little things matter. Seeds, sub-atomic particles, faery rings and precious things are often very, very small. And they often are overlooked, go unnoticed or are judged "ordinary" due to their lack of size. But such small things have power, magick and significance far beyond their size. They are gifts from the world of the faeries, and as such, the more you express your gratitude and appreciation for them, the more faery blessings and magick can enter your life.

And those little things are often "invisible". So when you draw this card in a reading, be sure to take a look around, both with your physical eyes and with your spirit eye. Have a delicate feel with your faery fingers, find what has been given to you and then give thanks for the little things in your life. The tiny things. Make an offering today for the faeries – a thimbleful of milk and honey, and create a faery bower. Clear a small section of the garden and let it be wild and free, for in that small area, they feel at home, more so than amidst the order. This faery here is protecting her sacred toadstool, a section of the faery ring that is as important as any other. So today, be on the alert for small signs coming to you from the faery. Perhaps a faery ring has sprung up near your home or in your garden. Protect it, and leave an offering near it.

Faeries are oft-times tiny, but they are very strong. They stop roadworks destroying sacred rings. They whisper in the ears of earth guardians and wildlife warriors, asking them to protect trees and animals. They, being tiny and often invisible to others, are underestimated and often misunderstood. They are powerful beings, and though some are tiny and appear as little more than a flicker of light from the corner of your eye, or a sense that something just flew behind you, they are strong, wild, and assisting us greatly.

So today, notice what is overlooked. Do something "small" and know that though your life itself may seem small at times, it is a powerful and magickal one, and you too can bring many blessings to both the planet and the soul of nature.

The butterfly lives for a short time span – a day. Perfect poems can be small. There are perfect minutes of music, just as there are day-long operas. Sometimes there is something exquisite in scaling down what we do and creating something precious and shining, in getting closer. See what can be "reduced" in your life and know that it will shine the brighter for this seeming reduction.

Divinatory Meanings

Modesty. A deliciously small sense of scale. Miniatures. Natural beauties that may only last a few minutes. Dew on the grass. A rainbow in a crystal. A brief and gentle breeze on a warm summer's day. A reflection on water. A delicious strawberry and a flower in bloom. A light moving on the periphery of your vision, signifying faery contact. All these things are precious. Today, make an offering and give thanks for a small treasure within your life. Be generous in your appreciation. Keep things small and beautiful. Something needs to be "in miniature" to be at the right size. Do not criticize something, a gentle tendril of new plant pushing through soil, for not being large in size yet. Break down a task into its smaller components and take baby steps. Give thanks for each small step along the way. Know that over the magick of time, small things grow. Know that some things are better for being small. They are not meant to become "big". They are tiny and they are treasures. Being pushed to make something "bigger," louder and more noticeable. Small is the way to go for now. Look closer and at the detail. Understand the power of gratitude in terms of growth. Know your life is in some ways small and very precious because of this.

Reversed Meanings

Underestimating the significance of a "small start." Overlooking details, being overwhelmed by the big picture and not understanding its components. Wanting things to be bigger, grander, more "noticeable." Feeling resentment for being overlooked. Wondering if anyone notices the thousand small things you do that create a life. Overlooking the small things another does. Walking over or through treasures, like faery rings, and destroying something precious. Insensitivity to the little things.

21. Crystal Magic

Creation, Dawn, The beginning

In the beginning, there was one faery, and a crystal chamber where all the souls of the world would be birthed… and she danced, and drew forth from one shining stone a soul, which she blessed and set free into the world…

This is the faery of creation, of the very beginnings of all things. Of the source, of the thought, of the spark, of the birth and of the magick of your connection to the Source.

This faery being is dancing into existence the song of the crystals, the form of the crystals. Within each of those crystals is a soul, which when birthed, will be you, and me, and we, and all. The dance of creation is an endless, lifetimes-long song, with drifting harmonies and changes in rhythm from lifetime to lifetime, and we are all birthed from the same place, a place of source. We are all part of this divine connection, and we all have within us that flame, that is our star-fire, our connection to the All-That-Is. This faery asks you to remember that whoever you seem to be, there is a larger, more transpersonal part of who you are, a part of you that belongs within All-That-Is. And while you have individual expression of it this lifetime, you are indeed beyond knowing in a human sense. And this faery being's role is to sing the song, to dance the dance that reminds us all of our star-fire and our common origins.

She dances alone, and from each movement springs golden tendrils of energy, running from hands, through feet, whirling around and through her, a weaving of energies that calls souls back into life. And as long as she dances, shaping the source into patterns that we recognise as life forms, there will be happiness, and merriment, and the ecstasy of being. And the crystals sing, and life comes again.

Divinatory Meanings

Creating your own world. The end of chaos. Freedom to choose. Singing your own song. Freedom of movement. Grace and meaningful activity. Beginnings to new ventures that are divine. The origins of a new venture. The ability to heal or amplify energy crystals. Working with true energy, dance and movement to express yourself. Healing through sound, crystals, dance and energy. Ecstatic movement. Dancing as if you are alone – no self-consciousness, no guilt, total bliss in being.

Reversed Meanings

Refusing to look beyond the ramifications of this lifetime. Seeing yourself as your personality and physicality alone. Not understanding that your experience is as a unique part of the energy that is All-That-Is. Believing in a father-God figure and seeking his love and approval, rather than going beyond into the mystery of existence and the joy of being here. Seeing yourself as locked into this lifetime alone. Limiting beliefs of self. A refusal to love the possibilities of your life. A firm belief in limits and shortcomings. Limited physical movement. Resistance to connecting with sacred sound and movement. Seeing the physical as non-spiritual.

22. Snail's Pace

Slow down, Grounding, Listen for the heartbeat of the earth, Subtle energies

This beautiful faery is entranced by the graceful, slow-motion movement of her friend the snail. She observes each movement forward and understands how far he comes, though in comparison to her, he moves slowly. She reminds us that we all travel at our own pace and that there is much to be said for taking time to slow right down and observe the signs around us. This snail has the time to converse with the faery: to have conversation, to share, to show. She has not rushed through this encounter and she has become quiet, centred and observant as a result. In this space you are able to discern what is truly taking place and read the signs around you. When all is rushed and hurried, when all is the barrage of smells and light and shocks that our world can be, slow movement can seem less vital. But she asks you now to slow down, to sit down on your mother the earth and watch the life of her creatures. As you do, know that you too are one of her creatures, and one of your roles is to read the signs and the movements of all creatures, no matter how humble.

Please understand that you have the right to do nothing from time to time. Within that quiet, peaceful space comes fresh energy for inspiration, creativity and co-operation. Without it, we can burn with resentment even as we overcome our own hardest taskmaster. No one is in charge of you but you. You are the authority in your own life and you have the right to call for a time-out to assess your life. You may feel estranged from your magical divinity, but please take the time to re-connect and witness the peace and loving energy that flows in your life, creating loving communication, enriching work and boosting your creativity.

Divinatory Meanings

The faeries can see beneath the "shell" you present to others and they know too that you doubt your own impact and influence. But they look upon you tenderly and they wish for you to take this time to slow down, find your own pace and place in the world, and to go your own way. This faery's appearance signifies oh-so-strongly that it is time for you to find the path that is your own. While others may see you as lazy or even slow and a little foolish, that is none of your business. It is time to slow down, to check your pace and to find the rhythm that feels best to you. And know that you have a faery guardian watching over you, happy to see you moving into your own energy, time and space. You can be lonely at times and need to be aware of your surroundings. Your hard shell protects a sweet and soft being. You leave behind silvery beauty, an energy stream that is discernible to those who are sensitive — as are you.

Do not confuse slowing down for a time of stasis, as from this soft contemplation of a gentle pace, you will create anew. When you observe the creative forces that you have mustered together and released into the material world, you will realize that your thoughts have created the tangible reality about you. What do you see that you love? What would you like to incorporate into your life? There will soon be many new choices. For now, please work on nurturing, protecting, and loving yourself by keeping a slow and gentle pace. Pay attention to what is happening in each moment. Listen to your heartbeat. Feel it echo throughout creation.

Reversed Meanings

There is a feeling that you must push and push and push yourself at present. You feel guilty about slowing down and simply being. There is a feeling that you simply must fill up every moment of space. There is an opportunity to take stock at present, but you may be engaging in avoidance behaviour: creating tasks even when none truly exists, placing high expectations on yourself to never take it easy, and even holding others responsible for your self-inflicted excessive workload.

23. Follow Me

Come! This is your invitation to enter the realm of Faery!

This tall, strong faery queen beckons you forward, wearing her gossamer garments – the key to the secrets of faery. Will you follow her? Will you hesitate, remembering all the fearful stories you have heard of the fae and their kind? Will you feel her blood call to yours, and a golden thread run between you that draws you gently forward?

When the faery queen calls us, our response varies, as it is a unique response formed of our fears, our dreams, our truth and whether our wild pure heart has been ignited. If you have been in physical pain, this is an invitation to allow the suffering to pass and to fall away. The entry into faery realms will eradicate pain and ease your heartache. She is alchemy itself. Her hair the colour of the golden gift that comes to you when transformation has taken place. Her lips are red for the blood of the wise and the white is that of the pure self. Between her hands flows energetic magic – she has the faery healer's touch, and her energy flows between the receptor and the sending hand. If you have dreamed of this, this is your opportunity to embrace the faery self within, and to come with her into a realm where healing and beauty and joy are omnipresent.

And the truth is that there is no fearful price to be paid for following this path. There is no extraction with which you must pay. Those tales have kept us away from our faery folk kin for so long, and again and again they ask, will you join us? Love us? Let us heal you?

The energy of the earth, the magical energy of electromagnetic sea and sky and field and flower radiates from her. Her eyes shine with love and confidence, and her beauty is that of the natural world in female form. She is transforming and healing the world, as well as providing a loving example to all who encounter her. She can come to you as a vision, a startling dream, or simply manifest as the quiet strong voice within that whispers, "Come with me." Step forward and let her show you the wonders that will be unlocked with the key of faerie. See yourself anew, and glow as she does. She is about to share her knowledge. You are ready.

Divinatory Meanings

Faery connections. Second sight. Being faery-touched. Experiencing rapid opening to the subtle worlds. The veils between the worlds dissolve and you can see clearly. Increase in your gift. Healing powers increase. Belief creates reality. Knowing creates truth. Egoic doubts and cynical thoughts melt away and all is magickal and true. Seeing the path you can now follow. Connecting with your wild self. An urge to be in nature, to be with flowers, trees, fruits, plants and stones. Shy of people who are harsh and unmagickal. A realisation that there is no separation, only a refusal to believe creates inability to see.

Reversed Meanings

Is there a strong block, some fear and anxiety regarding living outwardly your intuitive self? Speaking your truths? Are you mistrusting the effect living in the light will have? Do you fear rejection from friends or family if you embrace your spiritual path, or that the power you sense you have is somehow unreal? The magician card appearing reversed in a spread can indicate that you may be disconnected from your magickal powers due to illusions of fear, of punishment, ridicule, a feeling that living your inner truths may be unsafe or a delusion. Magick is natural – there is nothing alien or bizarre about being intuitive and living magickally, reconnected with your power. Your confidence could be low, and you may not feel beautiful. The stars are within your reach – there is energy that emanates from you. Could your energy be low? Are you feeling drained and disconnected from your Source?

24. Golden Gift

Magickal help is on its way

Can you see this little faery whispering to her Queen all she knows of your circumstances? 'Tis time, she has decided, for magickal intervention and the Queen has agreed that you will be bestowed the magick of the faery touch. Her Golden Gift is yours for a time, and blessings are on their way, just as fast as this small faery flies back to your side. You may feel her fluttering by, whispering suggestions in your ear, asking you to read a certain book, visit a certain place, or even eat certain food. For the faery Queen is a great healer, and her gift is of transformation, which will come about in the most subtle and beautiful of ways.

When the gift comes, your energy fields will be cleansed and renewed. Negativity is clearing from your chakras and your auric energy fields, to be filled with a gentle, golden glow that shines brighter the happier and healthier you are. People will soon be commenting on your rebirth, how happy, how radiant you are. Your endurance will increase, as will your stamina, and what once tired and disheartened you will be easily dissolved and transmuted. Once you have received the golden gift of the faeries, abundance will be attracted towards you. Your creativity will flower, as will your energetic determination to see dreams realised. There will be no more denials or self-doubt. Anything of that sort will be but the faintest echo of the past.

Nature and her healing are now yours to experience. Allow your heart to open, be grateful, and give thanks. Make a small offering, and know that this woman of the antlers, this faery deer woman, is of regeneration and of shedding the past. Your feelings of sexuality and sensuality now heighten. You will now be able to give love and accept love, physical love, in return. Allowing your sensitivity to return. Falling away of armour and barriers.

Your happiness, your health, your prosperity, your sacred sensuality is calling you. Let it be yours, now.

Divinatory Meanings

A faery healing is coming; lifting and dissolving depression, bringing sensual bliss, calming your frustration and any anger you may have felt towards others who you feel have hurt you. Your emotions are stabilising and running fresh and pure again. Stagnation is leaving and you will now receive clear faery communications about healing modalities which will work with your energy. Wear gold, which will amplify the message of this gentle healing card. Know that while the Deer Queen is gentle, her power is enormous and her touch is transformation itself. Shapeshifting. Empathy with gentle forms of nature. Feminine power. Return of sexual feelings, of sensuality.

Reversed Meanings

Fear and mistrust of your sensual nature. Feeling that every gift must come with a price. Refusing to receive as there is no saying what you may be asked to sacrifice. Believing untruths that the faeries are unkind and callous. Fearing that to surrender into love, that to be in love is to be too vulnerable. Not seeing your own desirability. Refusing to be sensual. Refusing to own your power and work with it in gentle, powerful, healing ways. Not trusting your own sensual allure, you seek to smother it, deny it or say it is impure. Refusing the golden gift of love, healing and feminine truths.

25. The Grail Faery

Fertility, The return of life, Health, Life cycles

You have felt as though your life has not been flowing and a sense of being stuck has pervaded your days. No longer, sweet one. For as you see, this beautiful faery is bathing in the pool of the moon and holding up her magickal chalice of life to collect the enchanted waters, which will soon be raining on you, blessing you with their cleansing and powerful healing properties. With this water she will bless not only you, with the unfurling of dreams and wishes, but she will also bless the women who wish to bring forth their babes and the crops so they will drive their way through the earth to the light. She will sprinkle them on what seems to be dead and dry and beyond life, and renew the dormant life force within them. She knows that as she does this, she honours the turning of the wheel of life, and the cycles through which we all move. Maiden, Mother and Crone, all are sacred, and all have their time. But when we see this faery, we know that we are still in the time when our own waters will flow and our own cycles will renew again. The chalice will preserve and store the life-giving waters, but those who she blesses with this will bring forth creative ideas, babies, artworks, dreams, loving partnerships and be cleansed and renewed. The mothering energy of this beautiful faery is echoed in the shape of the moon – she is waxing and in the sign of the mother, and is able to hold, receive, grow and allow in love, fertility, energy and the life-force itself. You are now ready to take up your chalice, turn it to capture the flow of life, and then drink from it, fearlessly and fully.

Divinatory Meanings

Womb able to bring forth and nurture new life. The feminine sacred magick of bringing forth babies. Flow of feminine energy and moon cycles. Blossoming. Births. Serenity. Female beauty. The taking of sacred waters. The first and second second phases of the triple goddess – maiden and mother. Every birth is a new life, a new chance. Princess of nature. Mother as sacred. Experience and the wisdom of our senses. Coming back into the wonder and knowledge of your sacred body. Merging of selves to create something new. Acceptance and delight and love of emotion. Babies. New life. Flow after stasis. Drink more pure water. Waters of fertility. Allow healing tears to flow. Red and white springs of Avalon, Lourdes, sacred wells, rivers, ponds and bodies of water are being watched over by fae, and will assist you in becoming fertile, both literally and metaphorically, again.

Reversed Meanings

Retreat from sensuality and emotions. Distrust, fear of emotions. Disgust at physicality. Disrespect for the body. Female problems regarding fertility and organs of fertility. Placing intellect over emotion. A mask of society and mind. Refusal to connect with nature and others. Isolation. Intimacy issues. Mistrust of women, the goddess, nature. Division of self. Body image issues. Unable to accept the body. Ill health, but unmotivated to treat and heal the body.

26. Little Boy Blue

Dreams come true! Return of the soul!

Hope and promise are reborn in your life, as this beautiful baby faery brings you innocence, trust, hope and the proof that there are beautiful new things in this world that have not been conditioned into unbelieving. This is a new incarnation, either of a new soul being brought in around you or your chance to be reborn without passing – your chance to become as a child again and be born anew without the physical return to Source this time. This new baby brings union. People of all kinds of different worlds can be drawn together now peacefully, and can feel happy and safe with each other. This child represents the new world into which we are all to be born and in which our intuitive possibilities will be enormously strong. This will be a time of fast growth and incredible development. Do not see the baby as "blank", for babies grow and transform each day, renewing cells and energy, and are not closed at all to the wonders of the magick around them! They have no "words" as yet and so express themselves with perfect truth and honesty. They change and yet are utterly true to who they are. And of course, they are so strong and powerful! It is time for you to be as a babe in the world, to truly hear and see and know for the first time. To approach with an innocent heart. To know that being human is to be all, and is a great gift. And you, as are we all, are responsible for the children of the world, and responsible for helping them have a future on this planet. It is an awesome and sacred task.

Divinatory Meanings

Lighten up and feel joy, for your hopes are going to be given form, feeling and spirit! New projects are coming into the world. The discovery of a gift. Babies, children, innocence and laughter. Letting go of old concepts and ideas that no longer serve; approaching life with the open heart of the child. This is a card representing someone who is at home with their sensitivity and their psychic abilities, and who is able to help the world simply through being themselves, who they are at their core and using their beautiful, innate, intuitive talents.

Reversed Meanings

Feeling stuck at a certain stage and not allowing the new and fresh to speak to you, or through you. Not understanding that wisdom is innocence. A sense of wonderment seems a very long time ago – feeling old, worn out, tired and as though life cannot continue in the same way.

27. Carry Me Home

Support, Time to be carried, Allow others to help

See these beautiful beings? Can you feel the loving trust that lies peaceably between them? See how she leans on him, without shame or feeling weak? Without self-criticism and embarrassment? See the bliss on her face and the relaxation flowing through her aetheric body? And see how strong he is, how he loves her, and how he welcomes this time when he can carry her a little further on their paths? He welcomes this. There is no resentment, no pain, and nothing to owe for the gift being given at this time.

Now it is time for you to allow another to carry you for a time. To give to you and support you on your way home. To take this time to lift you up and move you further along the path. Because there are times in our lives when we are tired, but we are still happy, and even happier still if someone can let us rest, and carry us forward. In that happy, yet exhausted place, where we have done good work and fulfilled our commitments to ourselves and to others, you can finally allow yourself to accept the support of someone who truly wants you to lean on them. When we truly learn to surrender to what is, support in many forms will come. And that is what is happening for you now. Just as this beautiful faery man is carrying home this blissfully exhausted faery woman, who is locked in a romantic embrace with him, it is time for you to surrender and allow someone else to partner you through what is taking place. Because not only is there support, there is giving in allowing this to take place. Allow someone to give to you their strength, their support, their energy and their courage at this time. Allow yourself to feel the bliss of trust and fall into the dance of receiving and giving. Because when you allow support to be given to you in this way, you open yourself to even deeper love, eroticism and gifts between man and woman. Because this is the sacred dance. And there is no weakness in it. Only beauty, exchange and surrender.

Divinatory Meanings

True love is a dance of giving and receiving, and this time it is your turn to receive, to be carried and to be supported. So expect someone to make your concerns their concerns. Feel and know the love of the faeries through intense love of another, which is peaceful and soothing to the soul. Feel their strength and love, and feel the sweetness of allowing their support. Close embrace, delicious submission to love.

Reversed Meanings

Refusing the support of another, for fear of what you may "owe" after accepting the support. Feeling unsure about the terms of exchange of protection and love. Fearing that to relinquish control means to let go of your own self and strength. Seeing your own independence as a state which must be maintained, no matter how tired you are, no matter how far you have travelled, and no matter how loving it would be to allow another to give their strength to you for a time. Confusing the acceptance of support with weakness. For now, consider your beliefs around your own strength, and know there are other strengths and that one of these could be the acceptance of love and support when you are tiring.

28. Once was Innocent

Knowledge means change

Once you did not know. You did not know the truth that your heart belongs to nature, that you were born innocent and you shall die wise, and that this is the true natural law. Once you did not know. But now you do. And now you do know, you must decide what to do. For now you have seen, and tasted and drank the faery foods and danced in the faery groves and lain with your faery lover, and watched moonlight woven into jewels. You've watched water offer herself to the thirsty roots of trees for drink and heard the birds speak one with the other. Now you know of this magick, what will you do? Pretend to live as before? Endlessly go through the days, the next so much the same as the day before that it feels you are endlessly reworking ever so slightly the same time between sunrise and sunset?

Now you know. What will you do?

For there now is a choice, where once you were told (and you believed) that there was none. That you must grow old and die. That you must work hard at something that makes your soul shrivel, and simply tolerate it. That there is nothing we can do, for this is the way of the world.

But now you have seen. And tasted. And danced. And it was no dream. It was dream-like and enchanted, but this is how your life now can be. Truly dreaming with eyes wide open. Truly living and drinking in bliss. No guilt. No fear. No shame. Challenges, yes, but for those you have your courage and your gifts. But to believe that there is no magick? That would be to lie to your own heart and soul. For now you know. And now that you do know, what will you do? You know now that if you choose the way they told you, the way you believed in before you knew the other, you know the way that will look. And feel. That there will be less of everything. And you know if you choose the other, your blood will sing and your heart will open. And you will be in wonderment evermore.

I wonder, too. What will you choose?

Divinatory Meanings

If you are courageous, you can now become who you truly are on a magickal level. When you accept this part of who you are, and accept that this magick you have experienced is natural and good, you will grow stronger, more fearless, more calm, more effective and you will draw to you the people who can echo back to you these truths you have found. You will no longer mind not fitting into a realm you always feared living in, and you will know you can find your own path, tangled and wooded as it may be. You can no longer deny what you have seen, heard, felt and touched and been touched by. You know magick is true and real. And that wonderment is your path, from this time forth.

So, what to do? Ask for help. Seek advice and consult people who have had similar experiences. Surround yourself with knowledge, and know that innocence is not lost, and that your beliefs are not naive. Your wisdom is now telling your truth, and acknowledging your experience.

Reversed Meanings

Denial of what you have seen, heard and experienced. Telling yourself it is only imagination or dreaming; that perhaps you are mad and need medication to stop the visions and the joyful connections you feel. A sense that you must stay hidden, or others will find you mad, and seek to shun you, or worse, put you away somewhere where you can no longer be heard. You are not foolish, nor childish, nor are you delusional or ill. You are in tune with the truth of the magickal world now and you have seen. You need not proclaim this to all, but to deny it is to push away the truth because you fear no longer being ordinary.

Which you are very far from being.

29. Into the Woods

Stranger in a strange land, New experiences, Feeling uncertain, Transition zone

This beautiful faery seems somewhat fearful, as she moves into a time and place that feels exposed and perhaps strange and unsafe to her. There may be her animal companions – the small rabbits – telling her that all is well, and to keep going this way, but those of you who draw this card may find that of small comfort. For when this card is drawn, you will be in a time of transition. You will be moving between worlds – from one realm to another – and in that change you take yourself far beyond your natural comfort zone. And so it is natural to feel fearful, and to keep looking around, senses alert, wondering where danger could next come from.

But if we look closer, we see that while she is not fully at home, and far from confident, the forest is flowering and the reward for having gone through this time of trepidation and nervousness will be great. So she will keep going, through this exposed time when she feels awkward, vulnerable, conspicuous and uncertain, and into a time and place when she feels sheltered again.

And as she walks, something happens to her fears. In their place grow her fallen dreams; her shattered purpose begins to reshape itself. As she faces each guilt, each fear, in their place springs hope and faith, and she understands that her dreams can be recreated. She will walk on, and the world will cease to be fearful, but full of joyous potential.

Divinatory Meanings

'Tis time for you to move beyond your shelter, to fly a little further from home, to take a chance and go into a place where you have felt uncomfortable. Things will feel strange and uncomfortable for a time, but you will grow and change and become stronger as a result. This faery knows there are places she must walk through that are exposed and challenging. She will take great care as she does so, but walk on she will. There is no turning back. And there will be great rewards and flowering of talents and skills as a result of this courage.

Reversed Meanings

The reversed meaning simply intensifies the upright meaning in this card's case. Allowing fear to "freeze" you to the spot, thus making you more vulnerable than you fear you already are. Feeling as though the spotlight of scrutiny is on you, wishing to be invisible and to walk on your path without anyone noticing and questioning. A sense of not noticing that there are indeed allies journeying with you, and doubting that there will be any reward, except perhaps that of standing out for being different. Not knowing the customs and language, how you are supposed to behave in this place you find yourself. Allowing self-talk about fears and lack of confidence to override your natural abilities.

30. Far, Far Away

Creative daydreaming

Those who do not understand, who do not dream awake, will say you are being disruptive. Unruly. That you do not care.

But you know the truth. That as a dreamer, you have no choice. The dreams come and find you. And that is a good thing – a blessing, not a curse.

Pay attention, they say. They look cross, and think you are lazy. Distracted. Not paying, well, attention. But you ARE paying attention, aren't you? You might be imagining the future. You might be spending time in a glade outside, or battling frost-giants, or creating the world's most incredible movie. You might be inventing a machine that can fly between dimensions, and you might be wondering whether it is time to make up with a friend you have had a foolish argument with.

So, you see, you are paying attention. Just not to them!

And this work you do, when you are far far away, as this lovely faery is, is important and good work. Lots of clever things have been done in this faery time of far far away. Scientists have dreamed of formulae that explain how matter moves throughout the Universe. Philosophers have conjured up Socrates, who tells them of his daemon who sneezed once for yes and twice for no! And while everyone wants you to pay attention, especially the adults and the teachers and the bankers and the news people who all want you to put your lovely mind and attention on something other than what you are meant to be creating, we, the faery, think you should pay attention to your dreams!

And they would like you to feel insecure. So much so that you would like to stand under a waterfall after being around them, just to clear the fog of fear that surrounds them. You need to be far far away so your imagination can do its work. So you can make up that story. See that painting. Fall in love with the way that boy's hair falls into his dark blue eyes. Don't mistake the truth for the facts they want to tell you and fill you up with.

Stay far far away some of the time. The world will be richer, stranger, happier and more magickal for it. Remember, some of your far far away moments bring you messages from the future...

Divinatory Meanings

A tendency to daydream will be with you at this time and this daydream will allow you to create, receive messages, send messages and understand far more than you believe at present. Far far away; others may say you have a lack of focus; that you feel disconnected. Allowing yourself to be distracted by ego. Easily bored. Short attention span. Needing physical involvement to learn; too much sitting still. While daydreaming is beautiful and enriching, 'tis important to ground these imaginings with endeavour and with craft.

Bring in the earth element and surprise everyone with the beauty of your creations!

Reversed Meanings

Paying so much attention that you are no longer connecting to the flow of creative dreaming and time. Pushing away messages in order to focus. Hardening your mind and your imaginative creative self in order to absorb facts and "know" more. Believing that you can be taught all you need to know from an outside source, without allowing magicks to reach you on those breezes of creativity that blow in when they will! Mistrusting daydreaming. Being harsh with yourself for "losing concentration".

31. Beauty and the Beast

Unconditional love

This beautiful faery is with those she loves. They are friends, true and sincere. She protects them and they protect her. Yet those she loves seem so different to her, yes? But she does not see that they are not tall and beautiful in the same way she is. She sees their wisdom, their courage, their dedication and their hard work. She is brimming with love for each of her friends, and their appearance being different is something she truly has not noticed. That is the way with unconditional love. We all have within us this ability to tap into a profound source of grace and blessings. And unconditional love, when we feel its grace within us, is a blessing, not only to others who receive it, but to we who choose to experience it. Being filled with this love can help us to heal and can assist us in finding beauty in all places. It can allow us to enter into life. Know that love, when it is given as a kind of business deal – you give to me and I will then give to you – is not love at all, but it is a business transaction. That kind of exchange may seem to give us control, but it does not create love between all beings. Unconditional love does. This faery princess loves all. The spark of soulfire within all beings is absolutely available to her sight. Her third eye is open and stimulated by the magickal green stone, the same colour as her earthling friends, and she is under no illusion. Beauty is beyond standard forms and features, and love cannot be given for complying and fitting in and making deals. Love simply is, and she has learned the art of allowing herself to be in love at all times, and thus her presence is felt as a blessing and the world and all its inhabitants bless her in return.

Faeries love all beings. They just do. And you can too.

Divinatory Meanings

Consider that you can see with everyone you encounter, indeed, every being you encounter, a spirit-being – someone who has that spark of soul-life within them. Consider then that when your soul-spark acknowledges theirs, you feel connected to divine love, which sees not species, race, creed or "distinguishing features". It enables you then to work and be with people who you may have once found difficult to be around. Unconditional love allows you to experience your own capacity for love, which is joyous and fills you with happiness. To dismiss, to be in retreat from others because of difference or cultural beliefs and stereotypes, is to dim your own internal source of light and reduce opportunities for friendship and love.

Reversed Meanings

Consider whether you have taught yourself to reject others for their differences, or whether you may have a belief that love is conditional, contractual, rather than allowing love to flow through you. Giving love as a reward, withdrawing love to show disapproval. Measuring it out, as a response. Love inspired by status, appearance and offering, rather than by being with those who most deeply connect you to your own internal source of love. Repulsed by difference. Categorising people as "ugly" and not seeing the divine spark within all. Seeing love as a physical, exclusive experience, rather than a transpersonal, inclusive state of grace. Confusing unconditional love with being a victim, or allowing others to mistreat you. You have choice and discernment. Unconditional love asks you to come into divine communion with all.

32. Beauty's Truth

Beauty, Physical pleasure, Sensuality

Faery women themselves despise the fine qualities of their men. Perhaps, after a thousand-year acquaintance they desire novelty. But more likely, faeries love mortal men and women because, overflowing with love and rejoicing in all beauty, they have the immortal strength to embrace all that is beautiful of both races.

Beauty is a form of power. There is no doubt. Beauty has tremendous value in our cultures, and yet we see it as a gift given to the lucky few. In truth, all of us have beauty, within and without. It shines forth from within and impregnates our energetic body with light that draws loving thoughts, admiration, lovers and friends. Beauty is not the narrowly defined version sold to us culturally, and insisted upon by the fashion world. It is a fluid and changing thing, different for each being, and each being has beauty, for you were born with this quality. It is your belief in your own beauty that leads to you allowing this gift to work its magic in your world.

When this faery makes her oh-so-casual appearance, understand that you too have innate beauty. That your beauty exists inside of you, and now your duty is to see it, feel it and radiate it out. The world will be a better place for you believing in your beauty. There's no being on the planet who cannot radiate loveliness, who cannot connect with their inner beauty and then radiate it out into the world. Can you not see how beautiful the world would be if you believed in your own? Nature does not work this way. The sunflower does not despair for not being a rose. Let go of the criticisms you have about your appearance, and the unloving thoughts you have maintained on your beauty. See it, know it, and shine it out. Recognise its presence within you, and then it will cover you in a mantle of beauty that is beyond that of the world of forms. It is ensouled beauty, and you possess it, as naturally and as casually as this beautiful faery; as naturally as a rose, a sunflower, a rainbow, and moonlight. Acknowledge it and others will respond to beauty's presence within you.

Divinatory Meanings

'Tis time to harness and radiate your own beauty, and to realise that by acknowledging your own unique attractiveness, your own beautiful qualities, you begin to BE beauty. Your job now is to embody beauty. If this feels daunting, know that this is not vanity nor is it an attempt to fit in. It is simply coming out from hiding. The world will benefit and you will be kinder, sweeter and more generous when you believe in your own beauty.

If you are struggling with the truth of your beauty, sit before a mirror on a Friday night and focus within on love. See this love radiate out from within, and begin to glow. And as you do, watch your beauty grow.

The faeries do this, and there is not one who is not divine to look upon. Having beauty will not make you weak, vulnerable, vain or foolish. All these are clichés, and you do not believe in the lie anymore, do you? Faeries have no judgement regarding types of beauty. They are loving and kind and those who keep these same values are beautiful in turn. Do not deny yourself this form of self-love for it has much power, magic and healing within it.

Reversed Meanings

Believing that love of your physicality is vanity and that beauty belongs to some gifted by the genetic lottery! Internalising beliefs about appearance needing to fit into categories. Wishing to be "other" than what you are and denying yourself the beauty that was gifted to you at first breath. Refusing to believe that others can see your beauty. Denying compliments, brushing off sweet things others say. Feeling ugly and thus unlovable. 'Tis a lie! Invite the faeries in to show you your beauty. Let them tell you of where it is, and what your critical and perhaps conditioned gaze may have missed. Let them sprinkle you with their faery dust, to see how you shine. Then let them teach you how to do this yourself and you will glow with your own inner light.

33. The Merlin

Guidance, Mentorship, Teacher of the Old Ways

When the ancient one, the Merlin comes forward to speak with you, you are speaking with all the knowledge of the ancient druids who have spent time in faery lands for years, many of whom remain there still, including the wise mentor and teacher, Merlin. It is difficult to overestimate his depth of knowledge, his compassionate heart and his laughter. He is part fae, part human, and all wise and loving. He is a teacher who comes to you with a message that you must find a teacher who claims not to know all, but who can guide you to the knowledge hidden within your own self, which seems out of reach and obscure to you at present. It will be time to study, and to be "corrected" when Merlin comes to you. His guidance can feel stern to some, but because he is not always available for long periods of time, it is imperative to make each moment count when you have connected with this wise teacher. He wishes you to know that everything is your teacher, that life itself is yours to learn from, and he understands that the choices you have made have led you to him, for now, and that in time, you will part, and that too is right and good. He is ages old, and he knows that much of your wisdom, encoded in sleeping DNA, is also ages old. He gazes into his crystal orb at the end of his staff, and the wisdom of the stones, and their strength and support are yours to lean on. You may experience visions when scrying, when Merlin enters your world. His good humour is only matched by his determination for you to learn whichever way you choose. Those who find him a hard taskmaster are actually resisting life's lessons and he will dissolve blocks within you regarding seeing, hearing, feeling, sensing and even smelling the fae! Merlin has an incredible sense of smell!

Divinatory Meanings

As Merlin is a bard, you may be drawn to remembering and telling stories and tales of your own life at this time. As he is a wizard, high magicks will attract you. As he is a guide, you will find a mentor, and become a mentor in your own time. As he is a keeper of natural laws, you will find you are living in tune with magickal cycles. And you will begin to read and know the messages for a time with such clarity that you may shock others – even yourself! Growing older need be no block to wisdom for you will not grow feeble nor doddery. You will know what is wise and what is not, and the difference between what is worth your time and what is not will shine out in sharp relief.

Clear, strong messages and a male mentor with Merlin energy may be coming into your life at this time. Trust the messages that begin to come to you, and know you are a blending of both worlds. Hearing the voices of stones, plants, water and sky at this time. Seeing forms within nature, human forms – as that is how they can best talk to you at this time. Shapeshifting feelings; merging into that which you are most connected to. This is true and deep druid wisdom, wisdom that is strongly connected and loved by the faery realm! Scrying will work for you very well, and consider finding a staff. Take long walks to conduct and receive your readings and messages. Remember, Merlin is a bard, and thus he will often "speak" with you in riddles and rhyme!

Reversed Meanings

Refusing to believe that a teacher can be found, blocking the lessons of life, resistance creating suffering and repetition in your life. Blocking magickal messages and your own magickal powers, feeling confused about how someone who is not "God" in the Christian sense can be so wise, kind, and loving – and good. Refusing to take advice, even when it is good and kind and strong advice. Refusing to love your humanity, which Merlin knows is where your wisdom lies. Instinct and intuition divided within you.

34. Glimpse

Indigo, Rainbow, Crystal children – and beyond...

This faery is a scout. He is looking through the borderlands into the human world, keeping a look out for opportunities to glimpse people who have magicks about them. New generations are coming, say the faery wise ones, and he is so willing to share and learn from and with them. In truth of course, we are all magickal. But there are also children and young adults around today who are more open and ready than the generations preceding them. The faeries seek these beings, so they can establish connections with them.

These new children are easy to recognise, if you know the signs to look for. Sometimes called Indigos, these children are peaceful warriors and activists with a deep love of nature. They are highly sensitive and can discern very easily whether people are telling the truth or trying to fool them. Some feel they are an evolutionary leap into what we humans are becoming. Ask this faery, and he may say that the children he is looking out for are simply aware of who they truly are.

Others, older magickal ones, are more scarred. They have had years of being told they are not "normal". So this faery watches for them too, so they can be communicated with clearly and told that they are not mad, but clear – able to hear and see. These beings will return from this meeting with the scout with a vastly expanded sense of all-that-is. They will return from the meeting vastly more connected to their own spiritual truths. They will believe their intuition after this meeting. They will know when they are being told the truth and when they are being lied to – just as they always have – but they will no longer be filled with self-doubt.

Divinatory Meanings

It is time to cease eating fast food and accepting authority's messages simply because they are "in charge". It is time to find your own inner authority and to take action to change the planet in healthful, healing ways. Time to transmute your anger about politics, ego and repressive regimes by taking meaningful and peaceful action FOR what you believe in. Seeing straight through illusions and speaking your truth needs to start now! You have been "seen" by the faeries as one of the evolving human ones, and as such you are responsible to your own inner truth, not to any exterior source of authority. Refuse to be dictated to. Protect nature and gentle people and you will come into happiness and balance. You are part of a new world, one which we are currently growing into. The more honest and true you are, the better off this planet and her inhabitants and life forms will be.

Reversed Meanings

A feeling that one may need medication to "normalize" responses. A feeling of fear concerning your "other senses". Refusing to accept that human beings are changing and that you are part of this change. Finding it difficult to accept that you have a part to play in the change taking place on the planet at this time. Conforming, trying to fit in, being able to be manipulated due to fear and guilt. Accepting harsh punishment because you are "strange". Accepting a medical diagnosis of your abilities. Smothering your abilities may lead to growing feelings of frustration, fear and anger. You need exercise, organic foods and empathetic like-minded souls in order to fully flourish.

35. Star Dust

Premonition, Galactic communications, Beginnings and endings

This beautiful faery seems somewhat unsettled. She is listening, waiting, reaching out to the galactic web to try and put together pieces of the information she is receiving. For she has experienced a premonition, but as these things go for us all, we are never entirely certain of what will happen, and when. Only that something will happen, and soon. And so she reaches out to what we humans have called the heavens. She looks to the cycles beyond those of this earth and wonders if we are all in the process of major change, a change so profound we have not yet found the words to describe it. She understands that the premonition she has is about cycles that reflect those on each, but she is unsure what to make of what she is feeling and sensing.

So she looks to the night skies, at a time when there is peace, stillness, and quiet, and gazes up above at the lifeforms and planets and the stars and their galaxies, and knows she has lived beyond this dimension, and that what

142

might be reaching her is significant far beyond her life, magickal as it is.

As she gazes up, there are baby stars and dying stars. There is star dust, which is sent out by the dying stars, and breathed in by the nebulae and used to form their new star-selves. And she knows that she has been on these stars and that her feelings are from a place beyond this time and place, and yet they have great meaning for her now.

For this is a true premonition. It is not an empathic moment, where she feels the strange feelings and sensations of another. She has had a postcard from the future, and from a place far beyond her home. And so she waits, as all of us with these experiences must. And she knows that while her premonition is as ephemeral, as light as stardust, she knows too that it is powerful, and will create ripples throughout all time, and all places.

Divinatory Meanings

This card can signify a return to source, a sense of needing to rewrite the soul contract, changing and moving into a new stage of life, a new incarnation. In order to make sense of these feelings, you may need to be alone and in the dark to work something out. Receiving messages clearly and strongly, hesitant to act on them. Waiting patiently for more information. Seeking connection in the night sky – when we can see other constellations and galaxies – and understanding your own stardust self and origins. Thinking a great deal about off-earth matters, about life in the Universe, and wondering whether there are galactic beings connecting with you. Visions and dreams of these beings and off-world communities and civilisations. Light-being connections. Ascended master connections. Clues as to what will happen, but lacking absolute clarity means you are feeling you must pin it down to follow your instinct.

Reversed Meanings

When this card comes forward to greet you, it may be a time when someone is passing, and a time when something new will be born from this passing. You may be refusing to acknowledge this, or unaware of someone's changing life and times. Denying feelings that are deep within, and that seem to forewarn and fore-inform of future events. Dismissing them as too vague to pay any attention to. While you may be able to sense what is going to happen before it does, you may still be wondering what to do with such a nebulous, delicate source of information. Because you do not know what to do, you too often deny it, and thus events you could have avoided, or let others know about, come about. A sense of being cut off from your precognizance; out of touch or practice with your own intuitive gifts, looking too closely for meaning, or in too bright and busy a place. Let the musing come in at night-time and information will flow through more easily and clearly.

36. Child of the Moon

Forgiveness, Transcending the ego

It is time to allow the cycles of time, the tides and the flow of life herself, and even the power of the moon's cleansing light to help you to forgive someone. For if you are suffering right now, it must be due to a feeling of resentment or dislike that remains within you. There is nothing that forgiveness and her power cannot heal. But how to do this, when life seems to flood us with memories of incidents that have wounded us?

This beautiful faery is clearing her energy within the healing light – the reflected solar energy of the crystal moon.

If we place ourselves under the healing light of the moon, our inner energy centres, known as the chakras – and there are many more than seven – are bathed with her light. As the mineral makeup of the moon is very heavy in crystals, it is incredibly healing to lie out under her light and release to her our angers and resentments – what we need most to let go of. Peridot is a crystal that the moon is made up of – geologists or selenologists would refer to this as olivine. Peridot eases out, teases out and gently lifts away from our chakra system, our physical cells and our light body any wounding energies that are causing us to think and feel anger. Peridot will also respectfully assist us to acknowledge where our ego is involved.

Please do not think the faeries are condemning your ego for they know that in many ways, your ego assists you, helps you live and can be a beautiful helper. But your ego can and will sometimes interfere with your wellbeing, out of the misguided attempts it makes to protect you.

Peridot also helps us reconnect with our destiny and purpose – issues about which the ego can be somewhat dismissive. If you take the time to be out under moonlight when you receive this card, and release to either a waning or full moon your sadnesses, hurts and griefs, your woundings will become your initiations into greater wisdom, allowing you to transcend the pain of hurts and move into the wisdom of experience and the bliss of knowledge of who you truly are.

This angelic faery is a child of the moon and thus the bringer of forgiveness.

Divinatory Meanings

You must conduct a forgiveness ceremony as sincerely as you can in order not to recreate a situation that has previously hurt you. While you are still vibrating to the energy of the past, it cannot help but repeat itself, even if the echoes do grow fainter. You can attain enlightenment – a lessening of the burdens, a reduction in grief, a return of good cheer and optimism – through forgiveness. By forgiving those who have hurt or persecuted us, we allow ourselves to be free. It is only then your repeating of the same cycle can be done with. When you receive this card, ask the faeries to assist you, to help you find the opportunities to exercise your forgiveness muscles. Ask them to help you clear under moonlight, and watch them clear and brush from you all the debris that causes you pain. Just volunteer for this. Just allow it to happen. Just be willing, be open to it. Then it cannot help but free you from the past and allow you to step into the present. You will know you have forgiven when reminders of the person or situation no longer cause you distress. You will see the blessings and the lesson, and you will not allow this to take place again because forgiveness frees us from the shackles of pain that tie us to the past and to people we have long left behind. When we do not forgive, we are, energetically and quite literally, dragging them around behind us. And it is that weight that can hold us back from our true potential.

Reversed Meanings

You may ask yourself, how is it even possible to forgive someone who has hurt you so much? How is it possible to truly forgive yourself for "allowing" this to happen? Toxic anger can feel righteous and just, and is often wielded as worthy and right to have. However, this moral certitude and high ground often cloaks a desire for vengeance and a misunderstanding of the nature of the relationship. Whenever a reminder of the person or situation surfaces, you know you have not forgiven when pain appears in the form of memories that still have the power to hurt.

37. Keeper of Secrets

Use your discernment, Confide in a trusted friend, Keep silent about knowledge

Patience, sweet one. Patience. This is a time to use your discernment and stay quiet. And if you must speak, speak only to a trusted friend. We here have observed humans and their increasing hurry and fret, their inability to wait for the right moment, to speak and speak, and not keep silent when a change is coming. And that is where I come in. The key will not be given 'til you are ready and you will only be ready when you have learned the lessons. To Know. To Dare. To Will. And to Keep Silent. Keeping silent is not the keeping of secrets as you so often understand it to be – withholding to shore up power within one soul – oh no. The silence is to give the magick the time to grow, the space to mature, and then at the right moment, the key is given. When you have sought not the approval of others nor dissipated your magicks with words, words, words, the time comes for us to grant you the key. For then we know you are to be trusted. And our trust is a great gift indeed. Powerful, magickal, deep, and ever-lasting. So use your discernment. Tune in. And decide wisely with whom, and where, and when you will share this knowledge. For it is our very life force itself.

Divinatory Meanings

You are learning to treat something carefully and with wisdom. Deciding who to share your own experiences and thoughts with is an important step in knowledge, for when you squander your own precious thoughts upon those you know cannot understand, you are allowing your own precious magick to be diminished and diluted. You are learning who to trust with deeper, more sacred moments in your life and your magicks, and who to stay quiet with. Learning the value of hard-won crafting, as opposed to the fiery genius of initial ideas, and enjoying the process of the in-between times without talking too much of them. Observing the 90/10 rule – do ninety per cent, speak ten. This way your dreams and magicks will live and breathe in life indeed. Be steady and quietly strong in the course of your love, rather than impulsive and thus wasting your magicks. So much of the magick is made by turning up and crafting something, simply by doing the work, and it's so hard to convince people of that, and it doesn't make the magick any less for it.

Reversed Meanings

You are tempted to tell everyone about your exciting news, discovery or breakthrough, and while this is easy to understand, it is not wise to do. Because with every word you speak before the work is done, you send away a little of our faery magick. You dilute our power to help just a little. You need you to act first and speak later. We also wish to tell you that the people you wish to speak to may not the best to confide in. If you must share these secrets you are learning, choose well, for these secrets are powerful and must not be squandered.

38. Greenman's Bride

Sacred union, Commitment ceremony,
Maturing into deep relationship

The Greenman, the wild heart of the masculine, has found his Bride, the beloved who is able to be both intimate and free. From their new love, true connection has grown, and now they are preparing to celebrate their joining under the heavens and upon the earth. For when this love is developed and grown, there comes a time to make a commitment of the heart – the kind that comes when a relationship or partnership has reached the stage where some kind of sacred ceremony will take it forward into a greater, richer place, where maturity and growth will be given fertile ground to work in, and where what you create together will have foundation, roots, solidity. For this card speaks of the wedding ceremony between the Greenman and the bride – and this takes both into a new stage of their relationship. No longer are they fresh and green, giddy from the euphoria of new love. Their love is deeper, richer and has taken on a strong life of its own. It is now time to sanctify this relationship by acknowledging its import to those involved, to make vows, to exchange symbols, and to join together at a deeper, more lasting level.

The wild man of the forest has found his beloved – and the innocent bride is ready to become a partner and a woman. They retain their wild fae selves, but they know they are ready for a long-term honouring of their love and their union.

Divinatory Meanings

There may be a wedding, an engagement, a betrothal, handfasting or commitment ceremony coming up for two people who are in love, and who are ready to take the step into their future as loving, wise partners joined in sacred union. Extension of family, pondering children and growth together. Contemplating the direction of a relationship and its future. When this takes place, the joy of the commitment between the lovers extends to fertility into the land, the turning of seasons, blessings on earth, and great joy amongst the faery folk, for they rejoice in love! Now, the balance of masculine and feminine returns with this commitment to honour the other, and to give and receive, in love, with honour, in sacred space. Work with the sacred oil spikenard when this card comes up, as it represents the exchange and honouring between masculine and feminine. The sacred union of partners deeply in love, and devoted. The proposal to develop a lineage; kindred, ancestors of the future and a new kind of family based on loving equality and honouring, physically, spiritually, mentally, emotionally.

Reversed Meanings

Not acknowledging the necessity of honouring relationships and balance of masculine and feminine. A denial that ceremony is of any import. Finding meaningless commitment. A lack of trust and belief in the potential of relationships. Unwilling to be involved in true partnership. Lacking devotion. Believing love is lust, and physical and short-lived only, or that romantic, committed love is a "faery tale". It is, but it is not unrealistic at all. It is our true nature, and we engage with ourselves most deeply when we love another in a committed, strong, free and blessed way. Short-lived, transient relationships. Guilt around sexual union. Fear of the self disappearing if committed to another.

39. Shimmer

Glamour, Confidence, Allure, Charisma

Glamour is a faery magickal ability to draw down around you, and draw forth from within you, the ability to gently shapeshift and cast a "glamour" about you. 'Tis the ability to shake off the dust of the road after a long day's travel and walk into the presence of the Faery King, standing tall and regal, with beauty as your mantle. It is not, as it is often painted, a false or untrue representation of self. It is a convergence of your higher self with your outward appearance, and is extremely powerful and positive in terms of negotiating your personal power. So when you come into the presence of this faery, in her court on her throne of stone, stand tall, and be who you are at your highest potential. Close your eyes for a moment, and see yourself being sprinkled with faery dust, from head to foot, and from within yourself, see this golden light awaken and radiate out. Stand tall and strong, and walk with deliberation and care. Meet the glances of people fearlessly, and with belief in your own power and worth. Be warm, and be strong. And when we do this, we come from a position of personal truth and strength, rather than from a belief in our fatigue, our "age, our infirmities, our injustices". We come from a place that Viviane, the great Faery queen of Avalon, would have worked with when walking into the court of Camelot to represent the Olde Ways. Know who you are, and then bring that forth: that is the true meaning of powerful glamour. When you invoke this power, all who see you will stop, share with you their attention, their respect, their time. And you, in turn, will do it for those who have found that power within themselves too. The Glamour is also a wonderful art for those of us whose feelings and thoughts are there for all to see upon our faces. When we wish to remain mysterious, call upon the Glamour, draw her down and forth, and remain within your own self.

Divinatory Meanings

You will soon be spending time with others who lead you to believe you are "less than". Be aware that in order to counteract the egoic tendency to go into your own "faults" you may draw upon the faery power of glamour and draw around you the cloak of enchantment. This will help you protect yourself from your own tendencies to submit to fear and sometimes not handle yourself as beautifully as you are able. The faery power of glamour is yours to be called upon. It will change your appearance ever so slightly – you will be more beautiful, your hair will be longer, more lustrous, your eyes will be larger and shine more and your skin will be dewy. You will carry your body with grace and honour, and you will radiate warmth and respect for yourself and for others. When this power is upon you, all will be drawn to you, and the glamour will get you through many a tough meeting. It is very powerful for when we need to ask for something from those in perceived "authority". Your fae appearance may also be emphasised when you call upon the Glamour.

Reversed Meanings

You may feel that you do not have the confidence, the energy or the appearance or even the "image" to handle a meeting or opportunity that will soon arise for you. But the faery wishes you to know that with the glamour, you can walk amongst any and be their equal. Glamour is not a mask or a disguise, but beneath its protection, we can observe and see what is truly going on, without revealing all. You may feel a little "less than" regarding your appearance and manner in comparison with others you will be spending time with but know that the enchantment of glamour is yours, that you can work this magickal shapeshifting to become your own, most magickal self.

40. Greenman's Door

Portals to Faery, Wheel of the year, Galactic and Gaian entry points

The faery know that there are times when the door to their realm is firmly, well, shut. They choose when and to whom the door will open. And while they may not look like they are on guard, the beautiful faery maiden swinging oh-so-casually on the handle, and the Greenman of the wood – literally – behind her will not let any pass unless they have shown they are good and wild at heart.

But what the faery also know, and what you are about to learn, is a great secret. For there are eight great doors to Faery every 13 moons, and they are as old as Mother Earth herself, and are powerful portals to other dimensions and worlds. Each of these great doorways and portals occurs throughout what witches call the Wheel of the Year, and they run from sundown to sundown of the following day.

You all learned of these times when you were very little, when you had time on your own, amongst nature, we faeries showed you the door, and told you when this door would open. You just had to know, and to stay aware. You just need to remember again when the doors open wide between the world of faery and your own. These eight special times have long been covered, or changed, or smothered by other lore. But now you know their true magicks, you too can experience the door opening.

Know that if you choose to connect with Faery at these times, you are entering a world between the worlds that is very real and utterly true, and can bring many things to fruition in your own world in "record time" as faeries are not impeded by our reckoning of days and nights.

Four of these doorways occur as the Earth Mother breathes, grows and changes throughout the 13 moon circle others call a year – and four are of the galactic web in which she is weaving our own earth dreaming and magicks. By connecting with each of the eight great festivals, you too will connect with powers of this earth, and beyond her. You will connect strongly with your faery self, which is both of this earth and beyond her too. You will be in tune with magick and by doing so, you will notice addictive relationships, compulsions to eat and partake of alcohol or foods that are not in tune with your magickal etheric earth self will fall away. These doorways, once walked through, can assist you in detaching from harmful thoughts and behaviours. Walking through these doorways HEALS.

Divinatory Meanings

You are about to pass though a potential doorway of time, thus you will soon have access to other dimensions and realities, including that of the faery. It is time to consider becoming a walker between the worlds, to draw back the veil and to part the mists. To do so will bring healing, change and powerful magicks into your current reality. Ask the Greenman and the faery maiden for permission to enter and make an offering. Then prepare for deep, beautiful, abiding change. Please see the front section of the guidebook for the earthly dates of the doorways. Make an offering, place your hand on the door, and push ever so gently. Then she will open.

Reversed Meanings

Turning off from the natural doorway points and refusing to walk through. Thinking you may be unworthy, and thus saying to yourself "Perhaps later, perhaps another time, perhaps when I am wiser, better, when I have studied more". Fearing what may lie within the world beyond the portals and doorways. Disconnected from the earth cycles and the galactic cycles. Feeling a lack of meaning and magick about you, though allowing yourself to be disconnected. Too much "civilisation" disconnects us. 'Tis time to turn off the electric lights and wander into the twilight to find your magicks again. Choosing the "wrong time" to enter the realm of faery, thus believing that the door is not opened to you; alternately, banging or pushing on a door and demanding to be let in cannot work with faery. Only timing, coming from the wild heart, and allowing will open the door.

41. Mother and Daughter

Mothering, Teaching, Sharing knowledge, Nurturing self-worth

When you become parents and when your children begin to ask you questions, what shall you tell them? We ask you now to be honest with your children, no matter how silly it may seem to those other grown-ups, because telling what you believe to be true is more important than you know. When you do this, you will begin to realise that being a parent is about teaching, as much as it can also be about protecting, loving and providing for a being. Of course, these things must all be done with love. But how do you teach the young ones the truth about the magickal world? How do you stay real, and true, and yet allow them to be free to experience the world as it is for them?

This beautiful faery mother is teaching her child the best way possible. By being with her child out in nature, she is teaching her child to hear the voices of the humans (some faeries feel *we* do not exist!) and to listen for the wind, to smell the scent messages of the flowers as they speak with each other, to see the expressions and feelings of the animals, and to know all that is around her. It is in the meadow, by the creek, under the trees, by the sea-shore that our children learn best. And by listening to them, we too learn in turn. You can transfer energy, and love, and teachings through a hug and a kiss. And this is what children need – for their teachers, their mothers, their fathers to hold them safe, love them well, and listen to their words with acceptance, without correction and complaint.

Divinatory Meanings

Time to spend an afternoon with your parents and or children, to take them somewhere natural and teach them gently the ways of the faery world. Do this through connection with the earth and what springs from her, the sky and what flies through her, the sea and what swims beneath, and the fiery sun and what grows from her power. (Yes indeed – the sun is Goddess too! Think of Grian, the Irish dragonfae Goddess of solar energy.) Think about how to teach your children how to be themselves. Offering opportunities for natural wisdom being learned. Offer to spend time with children teaching meditation, flower lore, nature-loving and animal wisdom. Let your mother and father know you think of them, and care for them, and thank them for their teachings, in whatever form they came. Love your children, and know you are their most important teachers – ever.

Reversed Meanings

Somewhere, children are being starved for this natural love and attention. Your own inner child may long to be held in the arms of a magickal mother who will teach you all she knows of the planet and beyond and this great magick, and yet you may not find her. Feeling alienated from mothers and other females, a feeling of separation from your own birth family. Never having been taught the ways within the family, there may be conflict around your own spiritual discoveries due to fearful conditioning and traditions. Know there are other ways and truths, and it is your right to parent yourself through this new natural learning time.

42. Dragon's Pet

Communication between species, Animals, Pets,
Magical companions, Guardianship

If this card has chosen to come and speak with you, it would seem that at this time you are nearing a relationship with the fae, moving into the realm where they dwell, and over which they have stewardship. Faery beings do not have a concept of owning the land, flowers, fields or "things". When they say "this is ours" it is nearer to a concept of this is "me" than what we humans have developed in terms of ownership and rights to do with as we wish. The guardianship you have over a certain area gives you responsibilities and it includes being as much owned by the land as you own it. It is a reciprocal relationship, symbiotic, and neither can flourish without the help and love of the other. Faery too have areas over which they watch, and in this beautiful image, a small dragonfae being has connected with a faery, and is reporting to her what is taking place on the borders of faery. What is being shared may be that a human one has come to share and to learn, or that someone (perhaps you) has asked to come closer to their realm. It is up to this faery and to the dragonfae being whether or not more is revealed to you at this point.

This card also speaks softly of the relationship between beings. This faery is the dragonfae being's "pet" as much as he is hers. They belong each to the other. In this faery concept of mutual relationship we can find fertile ground for our own companions and friendships with beings who we often call pets, but with whom we share deep bonds. We are not owners: we are guardians. This card reminds us to be worthy of that role, whether it be of the land, the flowers, the air, or beings such as beautiful friends in the forms of dogs, birds, or other beings who have chosen to share their lives with us. This card reminds us to listen to them. They will alert you to what is taking place on the boundaries well before you will ever know.

Divinatory Meanings

You have "watchdog" energy around you – a pet, animal or plant ally is relaying information to you. Please tune in and listen to what is being shared with you. You will know when energy is changing around the borders of what is called your home or land, in time to take positive and perfect action. A dog may bark at a person or being it does not trust, for example. A plant may wither after a certain being has visited. All of these are strong messages from your companions and allies, and the faeries communicate with them all the time. If you wish to connect with the fae, your companions are one of the first sources you may turn to to deepen and strengthen that connection, for they already have it and are already sharing those messages with you. Boundaries. Receptivity. Messengers from the animal or magickal world are flying between you and the fae.

Reversed Meanings

Being distracted and dismissive of messages reaching you from your animal companions, plant allies, from the wild or those who choose to share their lives with you. Not understanding that their perception is different to your own, and oftentimes more powerful. Not understanding the messages the faeries are sending you via your companions. Having a sense of ownership, rather than alliances and mutual relationships. You must develop your skills and listen to all that is with you when this card turns up for you in its upside-down form – don't block out the voices. Instead of reprimanding a barking dog, ask the dog why it barks, and then listen – really listen – it will come to you then – the voice of the faeries.

43. Midnight Prince

Ask for what you want – be honest!

This faery prince is a wish-granter. He will look right into your eyes, and into your heart, and see what it is there that you want. And then it will come true. Because he is a wish granter. And so, before you see him and meet with him, you must be scrupulously honest with yourself. Examine your heart and your head and form your wishes from the very best that is there. Do not try to hide your darknesses from him, or excuse them. He has them too, and does not find them bad, but he does know that whatever it is you want has been born out of all you are, and if you remain unaware of all that you are, you will have wishes granted that somehow echo those unclaimed parts of yourself. So, when you meet with him, and this card says you will, know yourself. Be who you are. And ask truthfully for what it is you want.

And this brings us to what you will ask for. Knowing that a wish will be granted, what wish will you ask to be given? Will you wish to be pain-free? To find new love? To be more abundant? What is it you truly wish for? And know that all the wishes that take you closer to who you truly·are, are the good wishes, as we humans call them. And all the wishes that take you further away from who you truly are, are the wishes that can distract you and go "wrong." So, do wish. Wish boldly and bravely. Truthfully and honestly. Because this faery prince can see all that you are. The more you know who you are, the more wonderful a wish can be granted.

Divinatory Meanings

If every thought is a wish to this faery prince, what are you on your way to receiving? This faery prince is making an appearance in your life soon, in the form of wishes and dreams coming to fruition. In order to create the greatest possible potential from these wonderful beings' abilities, be sure to know what it is you want, then to focus your thoughts, actions, emotions and intent on this. Bring all into alignment and be honest when there appear to be blocks, then allow them to be released, gently and without drama. The thing is to be honest about what it is you want. There is no penalty for being so, and there is nothing to hide or disguise about yourself. Only be who you are and watch the magicks begin to unwind in your life!

Reversed Meanings

Denying parts or aspects of self. Only wishing to see the "good" parts of who you are. Taking an attitude of denial. Refusing to own all of you, and thus the whole of your beauty and potential. Judging parts of yourself as bad rather than knowing their wisdom. Fear of making a wish – the saying "be careful what you wish for" has been ingrained in you, thus you are in stasis and now activating your life plane. Thinking you already know the whole of who you are and seeking wisdom externally rather than from within. Wanting an "external" wish to be granted thinking that will make you happier, without looking within and deepening your connection to the Great Song of life. Dismissing this gift of the Song as a hardship.

44. The Secret Path

An irresistible pull down a distinct path,
Ley lines, Mystical traditions

Faeries love country paths and wooded ways that twist and bend and take shape, but that are mysterious and very bright and dark, spooky and sweet all at the same time. Likewise, your own path must have both light and shade, and it is never straight! Faeries walk their paths to revive the land, and they take rests at special trees and wells, as do you, in your own way, create magick when you are true to your path.

When this card makes her magickal appearance, you know you are being drawn down a path that has the potential to lead you to a rich source of wisdom – one danced and sang and dreamt down by these faeries you now see. These faeries would have been spoken of in the old ways as "trooping" but here we would say they are following their path: swiftly, joyfully, singing and dancing their way to a destination that will be full of riches and joy, profound learnings and deep initiations.

These faerie beings are winding and dancing their way back to a sacred place: a resting zone for faeries to return to when the world outside has led them there. They will go within for a time, and feast in the halls of faerie; learn songs, dance with new steps, and then continue on their journey through the land. Though many faeries guard a physical place, there are others who dance the lines of power throughout the lands, and under the sea, beneath the hills and through the rivers, as the mermaids, whales, sirens, naiads and nymphs do. These faeries are dancing the lines of power that lead many of us to the sacred sites, and as long as these faeries continue this dance, we too will know where to place our feet, one in front of the other, in order to be on our path. Because our path can be something we reach by taking a pilgrimage. When this card dances towards you, you are being beckoned again to rejoin your path, and perhaps your first steps will be to wander a little, to travel, and see where the lines of magick within the earth herself take you. Paint your body with a little of the earth, and let the earth on you sing to the earth beneath your feet, and soon the song will be alive in your blood again. You are also reminded by the faeries that you can walk your path, be dragged along your path, meander from your path, slow down on your path or dance and be joyful on your path. How you walk it is empowered by your unique self's intent, and as you already know, intent is the heart of many a matter. You may find it is a winding path you walk, or a labyrinthine one, one which seems a maze, but here in truth there is always only one way to go, only one place your foot can fall in front of the other. Take steps again to be on your path. Reconnect with the song of the land that sings in your blood, and you too, like these beautiful beings, will be called home.

Divinatory Meanings

Ley lines, walking meditations, building or walking a labyrinth and journeys to sacred sites are all important to you now. You may wish to travel to lands where the olde ways are respected, to explore faery mounds, hills such as the Tor in Glastonbury, Newgrange, or Tara in Ireland. You will soon be welcoming friendships made by being true to who you are and being willing to enter into the mystery of the song of life. Joyful dance of connection. Loving, happy friendships with purpose. Travelling companions who inspire bliss on the journey. This card heralds a blissful stage of your life journey.

Reversed Meanings

You may be reluctant to start on your path: refusing to understand your connection to sacred places, feeling they are irrelevant, not understanding the song of the land and how it is sung in your own blood, fearful of meaningful pilgrimage and joyful creative play on the journey. Feeling that going uphill is too hard, rather than a source of deep riches. Fearing what lies beneath, as you may have experienced fear-based conditioning about what lies under this sacred earth. Confusion and misunderstandings regarding direction. Feeling alone on your path and uncertain about sharing your path with others, or creating magickal experiences with others.

45. Gatekeeper

Faery time, Time shifts, Dimensional slips

In both ancient faery lore and in the magickal world of faery, past, present and future co-exist, and are fluid and transferable. There are unusual – to most human ways of thinking – exchanges between these dimensions of time in faery, just as there are shifting qualities to faery space, size and shape. They are time travellers, shapeshifters and space travellers!

The most common view of time held by science, until recently, was that of Isaac Newton, of time being like a straight arrow shot forward from a bow. Time marches on, moving inexorably in one direction. We are born, we age, we die. Time, in this view, does not move to the left or the right, or up and down, and certainly never in circles.

But time indeed does move in a circle – in a spherical cycle which, when it turns, does leave behind the mark of a line. But the line is not time itself. Most humans do not like this truth. They prefer to feel that all is measurable, divided up into neat units, moving in one direction, and never changing within this world. It is, they say, a law. But the faeries prove this law to be a belief and nothing else.

You see, you too can break this arrow of time, in your life, by asking the gatekeeper if you can move beyond this law, or belief, and into the realm beyond. Time is not a one-way ride. And if you are prepared to live this way, then you will be more truthfully alive, magickal and experiential.

This is no new law – 'tis no invention. Ancient shamans have known that ritual or ceremony time is a place where there is no past, no present, no future – there is only now. In Buddhism, in Tao and in Hindu practice, time is not linear, but a circle. In the medicine wheel of the Hopi, time is a circle. In the wheel of the year, she is again, a circle. And it is in this circle that you can find yourself able to time travel, to bend time, to move between what seemed to be over, and what you can recreate in the moment of now. The belief in time as a line has led us all to feel we must control outcomes and destinations, but the acceptance of a cycle creates health, youth, beauty, joy and uncertainty, which is a blessing. The cycle of time does not merely repeat, she repeats with endless variations, and thus the faeries know, and wish to teach us that if we approach this with perfect love and trust, there are infinite variations on what we call the past and the future – and the now. For the door is perception, and consciousness rules your experience of time. And the gatekeeper will know if you are prepared to live this truth, or if the wonder of it all will be almost too much for you.

When we accept the truth of faery time, people reappear in our lives so we can recreate and reshape the past. We may journey back to a place where we have been and our future self can visit us. Seasons may pass in the blink of a blue-green eye and years of joy pass slowly. We may grow old, without ageing. We may stay young at heart and live way beyond the allotted lifespace the other version of time would have us believe in. We will feel the echoes, see the future and indeed remember how it is meant to be, and then create it simply by remembering. This may make life surreal and mysterious and there may be strange and odd occurrences. You may learn great secrets and fully be in the present. But you will always, once this doorway has been walked through, be in the time of now. In magick time. In faery time.

Divinatory Meanings

You can shape your own time, create portals between past and present, allow the now to be more effective and magickal, revisit the past and do-over when the gatekeeper arrives. Watches and clocks may no longer work for you, timers go off at strange times, there may be visitations from people you have yet to meet, and you may recreate your past in the dimension experienced when sleeping. Going to faery mounds and sacred places (stone circles, where trees grow in a circle, within a faery ring) may accelerate this process. You will see ghosts, and understand the future, and stay well amidst it all. For it is not chaos but truth, and it is not unreality but more real, more wondrous than any dream. Understand that the concept of linear time is irrelevant to the question you currently seek an answer to. Foretelling is coming to you as you tap into a source outside of the linear time belief. Understanding that time is a landscape and where you choose to place your attention creates the concept and experience you are currently having. Dreamtime of the aboriginal peoples of Australia is all time and no time, a beginning, life, ending and recreation occurring simultaneously. We too can dream and be without the time pressures we currently believe we need to experience. Some say that when we break through to the fifth world in the "future", we will no longer have this current time belief and all will change and flow. Once upon a time will be now, and forever… and we will be one with our ancestors past, companions present and generations of the future. We will speak and dream and share together.

Reversed Meanings

Refusing to acknowledge that time bends and shapes according to your perception. Holding on to control. A belief in moving forward always, at any expense, because to do anything else is a kind of death. Experiencing time's measure beating differently, but refusing to feel safe with it. Conditioning operating at full force in regard to beliefs around time. You may find it very difficult to be "on time" when this card appears reversed. Ask the gatekeeper for assistance and then time will be your friend and you will dance within its flow.

46. Faery Lovers

New Love, Courtship, Romance, Falling in love

Oh, new love! Enchanting and all-important, it is like breath, food or water. We fall in love, and all the world is lovely to us. We radiate a dense kind of golden glow, our brain activity changes, we find it hard to sleep, and eat, and our chakras are wide open and spinning and spinning. Our cells sing to our beloved, and oh, how we pine for them, even to be with them for a moment. We think of them all the time, for that is the next best thing to being with them all the time. New love can be stronger than the will to live – and finding love can give us the desire to live forever, with our beloved. It is not the same as mere lust or desire; it is altogether more necessary for our existence than either, splendid though they can be! When we fall in love, we experience euphoria, bliss and rapture on such levels that to return to a "normal" state seems wrong, unnatural, and like a denial of our love. Our chemistry changes and our dopamine levels fire up, leaving us feeling like we are about to receive the greatest gift possible. And we are. Love is sweet and powerful, and it is nectar to our own divinity. These faery lovers here have found each other, they are courting still and they know not yet the sweet rapture of giving in to the desire. But it is coming. As is yours. There will soon be flirtation, intoxicating interplay, and a flurry of exquisite energetic activity between you and another. You are about to be intoxicated, and drink of faery nectar, and know what it is to be alive fiercely, brightly. Fear not that it will burn bright and brief. This flame, if you accept the cycles of magickal time, could last forever. Smitten. Crush. An ambrosia drinker!

Divinatory Meanings

You are about to fall in love. It is most likely to be with a beautiful "other" who you will be spellbound by. Do not fear, they will love too, and the rapture that will come from this coming together will outweigh all the fear you have experienced, or anticipate experiencing, at its loss in the past. This love is new, but it may also be the experience of the revival of a deep, fresh love in a mature relationship. Courtship. Being romanced and swept off your feet. You will find you and your love are both magickal beings who respond best to being outdoors – making love under the trees will help you stay in love and experience ecstatic union. A wild, free, deep and true love is in bud! Oh, rapture! Oh, deepest and wildest of joys!

Reversed Meanings

Resisting what is meant to be. Being blocked in terms of your faeries and their guidance on romance. Being unable to accept the possibility of love. Loss of belief in new or true love and a feeling of creeping cynicism – a kind of rust in the soul. You may need to work on releasements in your cellular memory, past lives or auric field, and examine why you would wish to choose to give a past experience or partner the power to shape your present and even your future. What is it that you wish for? Be open to this possibility of new love and the blocks you have developed to self-protect will begin to be dissolved. Honour yourself and accept nothing less than your heart's desire. There may be a tendency when you receive this card in a reading to protect your feelings, to allow yourself to open up only as much as you feel safe – this indicates you fear that the overwhelming nature and power of love will diminish you, but loved truly, this power can only make you more. The harm with love comes only when we give our power away to another – your fear will not manifest unless you give away that power. If you wish to feel your own heart's potential, admit your feelings to yourself without editing or judging them and know that you can let them go whenever you wish to. The faeries passionately want you to know that love is a pure and powerful energy that is your birthright. Do not wall yourself off from its extraordinary, transformative bliss of the mind, body and soul. You will grow when you open your heart and you will be stronger, more beautiful and more in touch with the sacred as a result of it.

47. The Gift

A present, An offer, Nurturance, Growth, Potential

This shy gnome is offering this beautiful faery maiden a gift. It could be of love, of friendship, or a magickal present that will bring her new strength and attract great abundance. The question is, will she accept this offering? Because if she does, it will have many benefits. You see, gnomes are deeply connected to the element of earth, and as such, they are wonderful manifesters, able to transform the simple fact of earth into jewels and riches, food and new life, bright, strong health and glorious new love. As the creators and keepers of the earth's wealth, they may appear endearingly small and somewhat unassuming, but there is no more powerful faery being to work with. When they offer you this gift, take it seriously, for while it may look humble, it will lead you to a great source of magickal growth and potential.

When this beautiful card makes an appearance, know that a person or being who is very down to earth may be about to make you a good offer.

The more grounded you are at present, the better use you will make of this gift. Another being, who is often underestimated, will propose something to you, and while you may not think so much of it in the present moment, great things may come of this. The person offering you the gift has an urge to protect and care for you, to nurture your special talents and skills, and they truly wish for nothing in return except your good wishes and thoughts. Best of all, perhaps, is that this small gift will earth us, enabling us to ground, root and grow our dreams and desires. For those of us who are perhaps more ethereal and less able to take the time to grow our dreams, this is a most fortuitous sign. For instead of moving too quickly from one project to another, those of us who are unable to work well with our finances and who lack a feeling of being earthed, there is no more wondrous and helpful an elemental creature than the gift of a wise and learned (and rather sweet-looking) gnome. When given with such respect, goodwill and reverence, this gift will always assist you, as long as that which you work or cast for is in the best interests of Mother Earth and her creatures.

This gift may assist you with money problems, crystals, healing animals, gardening issues, tree magic, knot magic, fertility and any issues to do with brothers and sisters, especially twins, or people born on or near the same day.

Divinatory Meanings

A gift which has to do with your wellbeing, health and transformation. A proposal to help you change your life that is small and not in the least grand or glittery, but which has enormous substance and potential to it. Work with your hands – the arts of working with earthly elements is encouraged and supported by the fae: silversmith, blacksmith, jeweler, nurse, farmer, veterinarian, energy healer, animal lover, conservationist, builder or eco-mystic. Peaceful resolution to trivial disputes. The de-escalation of disagreements through tenacity, focus, strength, courage and thorough research and investigation. Reverence for beauty. Inspiration from the earth for jewelers, artisans and craftspeople working with the ores and stones of the earth, in converting our ideas into reality by revealing to us the practical elemental processes that need to take place in order for us to bring our visions into the material plane in an enduring and earthly fashion.

Respect for the innate usefulness of all things, which so many of us cannot see. This card indicates you would do well to take on the view that all has purpose – which is the antithesis of the disposable culture we live in now. Make the most of what you have and the gifts from the earthly realm of the gnomes will come forth in abundance.

Reversed Meanings

You may feel the urge to make a gift to another being, to whom you are drawn. The reversed meaning of this card may also mean that it is time to care for animals and small beings around you, who may need healing and nursing. Investigate alternative energy methods of healing animals when this card is drawn; simply search for a down-to-earth and humble practitioner of great integrity. It may be time to seek wise assistance to lose weight and transform your physical self in a practical, sensible, healthful and self-loving manner.

Lucy Cavendish author

Lucy Cavendish is a natural white witch who works with the elemental and celestial realms. She works magic every single day of her life, embracing it as a creed for personal fulfilment and happiness, and as a belief system that sees us as part of nature, and thus gives us all the motivation to respect and revere and delight in our unique experience here on Planet Earth.

Lucy is the author of *The Oracle of the Dragonfae*, *As Above, So Below*, *The Oracle Tarot*, *Magical Spell Cards* and *White Magic*. Her work has been enjoyed and recommended by beings as diverse as Deepak Chopra, Louise L. Hay and Fiona Horne.

Lucy Cavendish created Witchcraft magazine in 1992, the first magazine of its kind in the world. She is a feature writer for *Spellcraft Magazine*, *Spheres*, and has appeared in anthologies like Disinformation's *Pop Goes The Witch!* She appears regularly on mainstream and alternative television and radio, explaining the Craft and demonstrating magicks and the power of intuition. She is a classic book witch and adores writing and reading, listening to and playing music, connecting with the wild and creating enchanted workshop experiences. She is a founding member of the Goddess Association in Australia.

Lucy Cavendish lives in Sydney, Australia, with her pixie-like daughter, and their menagerie of plants, animal companions, spirit beings and beloved elementals.

Visit Lucy's website at: www.lucycavendish.com

Selina Fenech artist

Once upon a time, on the night of a full moon, in a small country town in Australia in 1981 a girl was born with a vast imagination. She was given the name Selina, meaning "Moon", named after the moon that shone that night.

As a child Selina loved to read. Her favourite stories were those of myth and magic, princesses and fairies. She soon learned she had a greater love than reading when she would spend countless hours staring at the illustrations in these books, ignoring the stories told in words in preference to the stories shown by the artworks. She would study each brushstroke, marvelling that any human hand could create such beauty. The images enchanted her, bewitched her, and filled her head with magic and romance.

Having always enjoyed drawing, Selina began to create artworks of her own ideas of fantasy inspired by the illustrations in her fairytale books, with goddesses, fairies and enchanted creatures, continually trying to improve and create that same magical feel and sense of adventure she knew as a child.

Many years later, Selina's artwork has been warmly received by lovers of fantasy all over the world. Selina still resides in Australia, being self-employed in painting her ideas of fantasy and selling her own artwork and handcrafted gift designs through her website www.selinafenech.com.

Her art has been published in books and magazines worldwide, and is available on licensed products ranging from t-shirts to stationery, figurines to jewelry. Her art has been purchased by customers and collectors in over 30 countries.

Selina's artwork is mostly mixed medium, as she always tries to choose the best medium to match her painting concept, and she is always experimenting. Normally her paintings are based in either watercolour or acrylics on paper, to which she also adds inks, pencil, pastels, and even digital elements to create whatever effect she desires.

"I want to live my life like it's a fairy tale, and I want my artwork to make other people feel the same. I love that for a person of any age my fairies can bring back the magical memories and feelings of adventure from their childhood. I hope that they also create new memories and dreams of magic!"

But all fairytales have a villain, a curse, a conflict to overcome. Not long after her 26th birthday, Selina was diagnosed with cancer. Luckily her prognosis was good. The cancer was caught early and is believed to have been completely removed. But the treatment and healing process of this life-changing event was indeed a hardship and challenge. It was part way through this treatment that she began painting for this fairy deck.

As Selina painted the images of fairies, and Lucy wrote, the deck emerged as one with a beautiful, powerful, healing energy. It is truly a healing deck. With each new artwork she created, Selina felt stronger, happier, healthier. The last fairy for this deck was painted not long after Selina had completed her entire cancer treatment. Her body, her mind, and her art had undergone great changes and growth during this time, and it is her hope that some of that journey, strength and magic can be passed on to everyone who comes into contact with this special deck.

"As an artist, I paint because of a true, driving need to create beauty and magic. It is an inner need which I fulfil by putting brush to paper. But there is no magic there until it is shared, no joy to be found in the forms and colours until they are seen by another. So I want to thank you, for looking upon my artwork and allowing its magic to become real, for making the image I have captured in paint and pencil come to life in your eyes and mind. It makes me feel a part of a greater magic knowing you now hold this enchanting deck, that you will share your wishes with and seek guidance from it for your loves and dreams. I hope that this deck and my artwork can be an inspiration to you. Thank you for being a believer and lover of all that is beautiful and magical. Love and Magic, Selina Fenech."

Visit Selina's website at: www.selinafenech.com

Oracle of the Dragonfae
by Lucy Cavendish

Features 43 cards and 164 page guidebook,
packaged in a hard-cover box set

In the not so faraway past, we were Gods and Goddesses…we dwelt in dimensional lands…Eden, Avalon, Ys, Atlantis and Mu…we were fully alive and fully magickal. We worked, loved and lived with all the elemental beings…but as time wore on, we were torn away from our strongest, most protective kin, the Dragonfae. Now they are returning to help us heal ourselves and save this sacred planet. This deck is a dimensional portal to allow them to re-enter our realm and deliver their powerful messages of love, healing and protection for a new generation of magickal beings…

Welcome to this journey through a world that has for too long been hidden from all but the most courageous of searchers and mystics. Within these pages, and on each of these magickal cards, you will be introduced to and given messages and wisdom from the boundless world of the Dragonfae, a world which is now ready to be seen by your eyes and experienced by your heart.

When we connect with the Dragonfae, we reconnect with the lost parts of ourselves, allowing us to fully explore the gift of life on this beautiful planet. They help us to access knowledge from deep within and reconnect us with the knowingness that we are all one.

Mythic Oracle

by Carisa Mellado & Michele-lee Phelan

Features 45 cards and guidebook,
packaged in a hard-cover box set

The Greek Myths are the stories of mankind. They are the reflection of human nature and human cycles and it is through these stories that we can come to better understand ourselves.

The *Mythic Oracle* brings these timeless stories and symbols into the modern world, providing you with a tool you can use daily to gently guide you through the cycles of life in matters of love, career, creativity, family, spirituality and personal awareness, allowing you to move through life's challenges with greater clarity, awareness and ease, so you can live a clear, focused and fulfilling life.

Exquisitely illustrated, the *Mythic Oracle* will give you deeper insight into what is happening in your life, what is needed and what comes next. The included guidebook features a description of the myths, their divinatory interpretations and a range of card spreads which will allow you to give accurate readings to yourself and others.

For more information on this
or any Blue Angel Publishing release,
please visit our website at:

www.blueangelonline.com